outdoor
europe

outdoor

Epic adventures, incredible experiences, and mindful escapes

europe

DK EYEWITNESS

Contents

Snorkeling in the
turquoise waters of
Croatia's Makarska Riviera

Safety Considerations

Outdoor recreational activities are by their very nature
potentially hazardous. All participants in such activities
must assume the responsibility for their own actions and
safety. If you have any health problems or medical conditions,
consult with your physician before undertaking any outdoor
activities. The information contained in this book cannot replace
sound judgment and good decision making, which can help
reduce risk exposure, nor does the scope of this book allow
for disclosure of all the potential hazards and risks involved
in such activities. Learn as much as possible about the outdoor
recreational activities in which you participate, prepare for
the unexpected, and be cautious. The reward will be a safer
and more enjoyable experience.

Introduction

Europe. Home of the soaring peaks of the Alps, the blooming lavender fields of Provence, and the glittering lakes of northern Italy—world-famous landscapes that are as iconic as the continent's cultural sights. But there's more to Europe than the usual postcard favorites. Here you'll find iceberg-filled lagoons and volcanic islands, subterranean caves and frozen seas, sheer-sided gorges and sprawling archipelagos. And that's not to mention over 450 national parks, more than 114,900 miles (185,000 km) of coastline, one of the planet's oldest forests, and a staggering 13 of the world's total 18 Dark Sky Reserves.

In short, there's lots to explore—but how? Happily, the possibilities for venturing into Europe's remoter reaches are almost endless. Across the continent, countless outdoor activities take you right into the thick of things. Instead of the restrictive confines of a bus or boat tour—where the closest you get to the great outdoors is watching landscapes flicker quickly past the window—there's the chance to actually step into the scenery, whether that's a sweet-smelling flower meadow, lofty mountain, or crystal-clear ocean. There are many much-loved pursuits, of course; Europe is deservedly well-known for its numerous hiking trails and snow-covered ski slopes. But the continent also serves up some more unusual options, including canyoning, coasteering, and caving—and those are just the ones beginning with "C." ▶

Diving between
continents in Iceland's
Thingvellir National Park

Left Mountain biking through emerald forest in Northern Ireland
Far left Paragliding high over placid Lake Annecy in France

Even better, no activity is off limits, whatever your abilities or experience level—this is a place where kayaking could involve paddling languidly along a slow-moving river or skimming over powerful ocean waves, and trail running could be an easy jog through a bird-filled pine forest or an epic, multiday trip across craggy mountains.

After all, outdoor adventure means something different to everyone. For some of us, it offers an opportunity to slow down, step away from our hectic modern lives, and reconnect with nature. For others it's all about chasing that addictive adrenaline rush, or relishing the satisfaction of a physical challenge. Whatever the motivation, the benefits are the same: being outdoors is scientifically proven to improve health and wellbeing, with even a short time in green or blue space providing a noticeable boost. It's no wonder, then, that more and more of us are hankering after nature-based adventures both big and small.

And that's where *Outdoor Europe* comes in. It's packed with ideas for getting a fresh perspective on the continent's remote places—from glimpsing the northern lights in Arctic Norway to kiteboarding off Cyprus's southern coast, scuba diving between continents in Iceland to climbing Europe's highest peak in Russia. So, if you're looking for a new take on the usual European getaway, go on—delve into its pages for inspiration and head off on your own adventure into Europe's great outdoors.

A wooden boardwalk
leading past pools and
waterfalls in Plitvice
Lakes National Park

Walking

Putting one foot in front of the other—most of us do it without even thinking—but *going* for a walk is something different, bringing a sense of adventure to the everyday. That's not to say it needs to be difficult—you don't have to scale a mountain or sport special gear for a walk to be meaningful. The simple act of traveling by foot is a reward in itself, no matter how short the distance or how gentle the terrain.

▷ PLITVICE LAKES NATIONAL PARK, CROATIA

Immerse yourself in the verdant beauty of an ancient ecosystem, where wooden paths and footbridges lead past flowing freshwater at every turn.

Plitvice Lakes National Park, on Croatia's Istrian Peninsula, is a spectacular oasis of 16 lakes linked by endlessly cascading waterfalls. Each season here brings something different: lush greenery in spring and summer, fiery color in fall, and a frozen wonderland in winter.

Formed over thousands of years by the constant flow of water, Plitvice was declared a UNESCO World Heritage site in 1979. Today, eight circular walking routes weave through the park, ranging from 2 miles (3.5 km) to 11 miles (18 km) in length. Winding boardwalks and footbridges lead you across natural dams formed by sediment, taking you within splashing distance of the falls. ▶

The Legend of Gavanovac Lake

Plitvice is steeped in ancient legends, such as the tale of Gavanovac Lake. It tells of a kind man called Gavan, who once kept treasure in a castle, away from his enemy the Black Queen. When the Queen sent a spy to find the riches, Gavan's loyal servant fled with the treasure chest. As he swam across the lake, the box opened and the treasure was lost. It is said that Gavan's riches are still hiding within its depths.

White-Backed Woodpecker

If you hear loud drumming from the treetops, it's likely to be a white-backed woodpecker making itself at home in a decaying tree trunk.

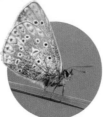

Alcon Blue Butterfly

This critically endangered butterfly can be spotted during summers at Plitvice. Despite its name, it's more of a gray color than blue.

Viviparous Lizard

Known for giving birth to live young instead of laying eggs, these lizards can range in color from yellow and orange to brown and black.

Ural Owl

Plitvice is home to a large population of Ural owls. These gray-brown birds are mostly nocturnal but can be seen in daytime during the summer.

Top Strolling through the forest on a wooden boardwalk
Above Looking upward out of Supljara Cave
Left The Kozjaka Bridge surrounded by turquoise water and green foliage

---∧---

Leave No Trace

Heavy footfall from crowded paths poses one of the biggest threats to the park, with plants being damaged and water contaminated. Visit on either side of the summer when visitor numbers are lower for a more serene experience and to help preserve this delicate ecosystem.

All of the trails can be completed in a day, but they vary considerably in terms of difficulty. The shortest and easiest route is Program A, which—despite its prosaic name—offers a greatest-hits tour of the lower lakes. Highlights here include Veliki Slap, the park's biggest waterfall, and the Kozjaka Bridge, a picturesque wooden platform that snakes across a series of emerald pools.

As you slowly meander through the dense woodland that surrounds the lakes, water tumbles out of the cliff-edge foliage, filling the air with spray that catches rainbows in the sunlight. Darting minnows leave ripples in the clear pools on either side of the path, while dragonflies rest on sturdy grasses nearby. Many of the lakes are named after those who purportedly fell afoul of the waters and never returned—a bandit chief, a Romany lady, a grandmother, a herd of goats—and it's easy to believe in such supernatural powers as you're engulfed in the cascades' perpetual roar.

The water may be firmly in control, but fragile life also flourishes in this unique habitat. Look carefully and you might be rewarded with a glimpse of one of the park's many endangered species, from the delicate, gray wings of the clouded Apollo butterfly to the bright-blue throat of the European green lizard. More than 160 bird species can also be found here, along with more than 1,400 types of plants that make the air feel as fresh as the water—the scent of soft mosses, orchids, plums, and lilies fills your nose as you explore. (A local company has even bottled the aroma of Plitvice into a souvenir perfume for those who can't bear to leave it behind.) Together, it all combines to create a rich sensory experience that will leave you feeling fully refreshed and invigorated.

WATERFALL TRAIL, SWITZERLAND

Admire dozens of towering waterfalls on a stroll through a spectacular glacial valley.

At Lauterbrunnen, get up close and personal with the Alps at their finest—towering granite walls, meandering cows, and sleepy, mountain-side villages. There's no shortage of serious hikes here, but for those with varying levels of stamina and walking ability, the Waterfall Trail to Stechelberg offers a much more mellow option. Wending along the valley floor, it takes you past an astonishing 72 cascades in just 5 miles (8 km). The most impressive display comes halfway along the route at Trümmelbach Falls, where 10 waterfalls have sculpted rock formations and a labyrinth of caves within the mountainside.

Top left Looking toward Staubbach Falls, at the edge of Lauterbrunnen village

MULLERTHAL TRAIL, LUXEMBOURG

Take a relaxing walk through Luxembourg's "Little Switzerland."

As you set off along the Mullerthal Trail, you never know what will pop up around the next bend: erosion-sculpted cliffs beneath blankets of ivy, gurgling streams flowing over moss-covered rocks or the gloomy entrance to a tunnel carved out hundreds of years ago. The full trail is formed of three loops that total 70 miles (112 km), but each is broken down into segments that can be walked in a day. And in this compact country, you're never far from a village complete with cozy cafés and walker-friendly accommodation, so a stroll through Mullerthal never feels especially strenuous. It's simply a gentle ramble through the woods.

Bottom left Walking through shady woods on Luxembourg's Mullerthal Trail

CAMØNOEN TRAIL, DENMARK

Stroll in peaceful solitude around a quiet corner of Denmark.

Most of Denmark is densely populated, but out on the islands of Møn, Nyord, and Bogø, you can connect with the country at its most wild. Here, you'll find the Camønoen Trail, a 109-mile (175 km) path dubbed Denmark's "friendliest trail" for the welcoming communities it passes through. The total length might sound extreme, but any section can be done as a day walk, with connecting bus stops part of a wider scheme to make the route accessible to all. Taking in fields of yellow rapeseed, sun-dappled forest, and quiet beaches, the mostly flat trail is a haven of tranquility, where the only sounds you'll hear are the rustling wind and a symphony of birds.

Top right Chalk cliffs along a coastal stretch of the Camønoen Trail on the island of Møn

MAWDDACH TRAIL, WALES

A ramble along this converted rail line reveals a beautiful Welsh landscape.

Having previously served as a rail track, the Mawddach Trail is about as level a walking route as it gets—great news for walkers and wheelchair users in search of a route with easy access. Following the Mawddach Estuary in southern Snowdonia, the trail winds 9.5 miles (15 km) from the medieval market town of Dolgellau to the seaside port at Barmouth. The scenery here is some of Wales's best, with the golden sands and cool-blue waters of the estuary backdropped by the forested slopes of the Rhinog Mountains. Much of the estuary is a Site of Special Scientific Interest known for its birdlife, and you might even spy an osprey as you make your way along the path.

Bottom right Barmouth Viaduct and the River Mawddach at the end of the Mawddach Trail

❝The beautiful Lac de Joux turns from liquid deep blue to hard silver when it freezes each winter.❞

Ice

Skating

Feel the fresh winter air brush your face as you glide easily across a frozen body of water. Here, in nature's snow-dusted playground, there is no rail to reach out for, no circular laps to repeat, and no crowds to be jostled by. Pushing one foot in front of the other, you'll discover the energizing freedom—and gleeful novelty—of exploring pristine frozen rivers, lakes, canals, and even the sea on razor-sharp, steel-plated blades.

◁ LAC DE JOUX, SWITZERLAND

Uncover an icy winter wonderland as you skate across a frozen lake surrounded by tree-clad slopes.

Forming a long section of the French-Swiss border, the Jura Mountains are not as high or as steep as their more famous siblings, the Alps, farther south. Thanks to this comparatively gentler terrain, this area is best known for snowshoeing and cross-country skiing. But the massif is also the setting for another winter sport: ice skating. Each winter, the area's beautiful Lac de Joux—nestled at 3,294 ft (1,004 m) in a subalpine valley—freezes, turning from liquid deep blue to hard silver and transforming into the largest natural skating rink in Europe.

As temperatures plummet from early December, sections of the lake are gradually cordoned off as they become safe to skate upon. By February, the entire 3.5 sq mile (9.5 sq km) surface is usually frozen over, and the whole lake becomes a giant open-air skating rink until April. You can skate from any point on the shoreline, but the traditional villages of L'Abbaye on the south shore or Le Pont on the north are good starting points. Here, there's a winter wonderland vibe: open-air stalls sell hot drinks along the lakefront—and sometimes even on the ice—and the surrounding thick forest lends a refreshingly alpine tang to the cold air. Join the throngs of families and friends out on the frozen lake and then, when your legs begin to tire, take a well-earned rest with a *vin chaud* or *chocolat chaud* and watch the skaters spin by.

Top Ice skaters gliding across the frozen surface of the Lac de Joux
Left Skating in front of the pretty village of Le Pont

A group of ice skaters
racing along Luleå's
gleaming-white ice track

▽ LIPNO LAKE, CZECH REPUBLIC

Go long-distance skating on a body of water so vast
it's gained the moniker the "South Bohemian Sea."

Fed by the Vltava River, Lipno Lake lies in the southwest
of the Czech Republic, a stone's throw from the Austrian
border. This long, twisting body of water is usually frozen
from December to March, its surface often velvety soft
with snow. During this time, a 7-mile (11 km) long ice
highway is cut through the drifts at the south end of
the lake, creating a wide, smooth trail that's perfect for
skating. Join in with locals taking their daily spin as
you glide along the track, hearing the whoosh of your
blades over the sparkling ice. Skating here is relatively
easygoing, but if you fancy more of a challenge, try
venturing "off piste." When conditions are right, it's
possible to skate almost the entire surface of this huge
19 sq mile (50 sq km) lake.

Skating along the smooth ice path
that winds across the frozen Lipno Lake

▷ LULEÅ, SWEDEN

Glide across the otherworldly landscape of a frozen
sea to explore frosted islands suspended in ice.

Sitting around 560 miles (900 km) north of Stockholm
on Sweden's east coast, Luleå is a likable modern
metropolis and the largest city in Swedish Lapland.
It's here, during the bitter Arctic winter months, that
something extraordinary happens: the sea freezes. As
temperatures plummet, fingers of ice begin to creep
across the brackish waters surrounding the city, encircling
the nearby islands and transforming the sea into a pearly
white landscape. When the ice is at least 14 in (35 cm)
thick, Jan "The Iceman" Blomqvist and his team leap into
action, plowing a 66 ft (20 m) wide, 7-mile (12 km) long
isbanan (ice track). The route skirts the city between its
north and south harbors and then strikes out to tiny
Gråsjälören island in the Bothnian Archipelago.

From mid-January to the end of March, ice skaters
of all ages and abilities—from locals pushing strollers to
world-record-holding speed skaters—give the track a
whirl. The section hugging the coast around the city
center is used as a shortcut, but for a real long-distance
adventure, set off in the teeth of the wind across the sea
ice toward Gråsjälören. Icebreaker vessels dot the
horizon, frozen motionless in the now-solid body of water,
and a cluster of white-powdered pines marks the island
ahead, offering the promise of shelter. Here, there
are wooden cabins where you can buy steaming hot
chocolate and warm yourself around a cheery fire.

Looking out across Luleå's icy landscape in the glow of Arctic winter light

Brackish Waters

Luleå's frozen sea is only possible because the waters around the archipelago are fed by freshwater rivers and are largely unaffected by the tide, which makes them brackish—more saline (saltier) than freshwater, but significantly less saline than the rest of the Baltic Sea. A lower salinity means that the sea can turn to ice more easily, although the freezing point of the water is still lower than that of freshwater.

Canoeing

Sitting or resting on one knee, canoeists use a single-bladed paddle to carve or steer through the water. The activity's contemplative pace—the typical paddler covers 2.5 mph (4 km/h)—is central to its magic; at this gentle speed, you notice sounds, sights, and smells that are normally missed. Equally key is a canoeist's sense of connection with water and that rare, low perspective—less bird's-eye, more beaver's. Canoes are a great bet for beginners, too, thanks to their open decks and higher sides, which usually make them difficult to capsize.

Enjoying a paddle along the winding, mazelike waterways of Upper Loch Erne

◁ LOUGH ERNE CANOE TRAIL, NORTHERN IRELAND

This trail of two halves takes you along the length of Lough Erne, a deep-blue body of water fringed by emerald-green fields.

Around 90 minutes' drive west of Belfast, Lough Erne lies to the western edge of County Fermanagh. The 40-mile (64 km) lake is split into two distinct sections: shallower Upper Lough Erne is home to a maze of narrow, winding channels and grassy islets, while further north, the island-dotted Lower Lough Erne is wilder, windier, and much more expansive. Linking the two is a snaking stretch of the Erne River, which flows nimbly around the historic island-set town of Enniskillen.

To explore this slice of rural Ireland, take to the water and follow the Lough Erne Canoe Trail, a 31-mile (50 km) long route that winds from the foot of Upper Lough Erne, near the atmospheric 17th-century ruins of Crom Old Castle, all the way to Muckross in the northeastern corner of the Lower Lough. While you could rattle through this journey in a couple of days, many canoeists take at least four; this slower pace will allow you to explore the forested islands, ancient castles, and historic sights that lie along the way. Happily, access to the lakes is completely free, with no license required. ▶

Insider Tip

Windy conditions on Lower
Lough Erne, especially on the
"Broad Lough," can create
waves akin to those of open
seas, so paddling should be
attempted only on a calm day
or by experienced canoeists.

Right Carved stone head,
part of the priory's ruins
Below The ruins of the
priory on Devenish
Island in Lough Erne

Much like the lakes themselves, the trail is divided into two
parts, each section reflecting the distinct character of the
lake it traverses. The first half takes you across the laby-
rinthine Upper Lough Erne, which more closely resembles a
delta or wetlands than a conventional, open lake. Moving
along its sheltered waters, you'll wind your canoe between
a litany of low-lying islands and miniature peninsulas. Historic structures take shape on the forested banks as you
pass, including the turretlike Crichton Tower, a 19th-century
folly built on tiny Gad Island. There's very little boat traffic
in this part of the lake—tranquility reigns, as does wildlife.
You might spy otters swimming in dense reed beds or the
iridescent flash of a kingfisher's wing as it darts overhead.

Eventually, all watery roads lead to Enniskillen, the trail's
approximate halfway point. Also known as Inis Ceithleann
(Ceithleann's Island), this historic town was named after a
fierce female warrior who, wounded by an arrow in battle,
died trying to cross the Erne River. Leaving Enniskillen, the
trail heads into the much larger Lower Lough, home to lonely
islands that conceal ruined priories, 12th-century towers and
mysterious stone figures. The route first weaves its way
through a tapered channel filled with wooded islands, before
opening up into the lake's wider, wilder northern section,
known to locals as the "Broad Lough." Tracing the grassy
eastern shore, you'll paddle toward journey's end, watching
black-capped sandwich terns wheeling overhead as the
sun glints on the inky-blue water.

▽ VLTAVA, CZECH REPUBLIC

Cruise through South Bohemia on a laid-back summer river trip.

The Vltava is the Czech Republic's longest river, flowing 270 miles (435 km) across the country before emptying into the Elbe just north of Prague. It makes for a beautiful journey by canoe—but a long one, so settle on the short stretch between Vyšší Brod and Český Krumlov for an easygoing two-day taster. Passing through tranquil woodland and past tiny villages, this soft adventure is something of a summer ritual for the residents of South Bohemia. Join them drifting languidly along under the dappled sunlight, stopping every now and then for a refreshing drink at one of the Vltava's floating bars. It's a relaxed ride—the only time you'll need to lift a paddle is to tackle the occasional weir. Eventually, you'll float lazily over the finishing line at the castle town of Český Krumlov, an elegant end to a couple of days lounging around on the river.

Paddling along the Vltava as it weaves through the picturesque old town of Český Krumlov

▷ TAR ROUTE, FINLAND

Paddle through the backcountry of Finland on a historic trading route that cuts right across the country.

Slap, sloosh, slap, sloosh. The dulcet rhythm of each stroke carving through the water is all that separates the silence. Droplets tumble from the blade, sparkling in the summer light, as you flick your paddle back around for another stroke. And another. Across the lake and onto the next, past forested islets and hidden beaches. Welcome to Finland's Tar Route, a remote adventure along waterways that were once used to transport barrels of tar from the Russian border to the Baltic Sea.

Starting on Lentiira, a tree-lined lake in the west of Finland, you'll spend several days tracing this isolated route, paddling your open-top canoe south to the town of Kuhmo and wild camping on uninhabited islands along the way. On some nights, you'll be pitching your tent in the lee of a wind shelter, hunkering around the fire as its flames send silhouettes flickering up the tree trunks. At other times, you'll cozy up inside a wilderness cabin, resting your weary limbs on real beds with—oh, the luxury—real mattresses. There are few settlements among the taiga forest here, and you can go for hours without seeing another soul as you cut a course along squiggly shorelines and down narrow rivers. Eventually, after weaving between the islands on Lake Kärenjärvi, the yellow spire of Kuhmo's Lutheran church will come looming into view, peeking above the town's treetops. Haul your canoe ashore and head for the nearest sauna to soothe your aching arms.

The Taiga

Two-thirds of Finland is covered in thick taiga, or boreal forest, part of an ecological zone that stretches from Norway to northern Russia. Taiga forest is dominated by conifers (mainly pine, spruce, and birch), which are clustered together in a closed canopy that becomes sparser the farther north you go, eventually giving way to Arctic tundra. Stemming from the Russian word for "pure," taiga harbors a variety of animals, such as elk, reindeer, wolverines, and brown bears.

Far left Looking over
the water near Kuhmo
Left A beachside bonfire
Below Canoe resting on
a sandy beach next to the
Tar Route's Lake Lentua

Wildlife Watching

While Europe might not have Africa's vast savannas or the lush rainforests of Central and South America, you can still enjoy plenty of spectacular wildlife sightings here. Whether you're scouring the ground for tracks or waiting quietly in a hide, all you need is a bit of patience, the right guidance, and just a tiny sliver of luck.

▷ SVALBARD, NORWAY

Roam across the sea ice in search of a polar bear, the largest land-based carnivore on Earth.

Marooned in the Arctic Ocean, midway between Norway and the North Pole, Svalbard is an island chain of extremes. Winter here brings perpetual darkness, summer the unending daylight of the midnight sun. For much of the year, the landscape is frozen in a white canvas of glaciers and ice. And on the fringes of Longyearbyen, the northernmost town in the world, road signs warn not of crossing children but of polar bears.

As its name suggests, *Ursus maritimus* spends most of its life on sea ice, roaming vast distances on the hunt for seals. Hop on a snowmobile and head out into the wilderness with an expert guide, your destination the frigid east coast. Weighing up to 1,765 lb (800 kg) and measuring up to nearly 10 ft (3 m) long, polar bears are easy to spot on the thick ice floes—from a safe distance, of course.

Right A young male polar bear on the edge of the ice
Below Safely observing a female bear and her cub

A female brown bear and three cubs in a meadow in Kainuu Forest

△ KAINUU FOREST, FINLAND

Among the fragrant pines and sprawling lakes of the Finland–Russia borderlands, you'll find hungry bears searching for supper.

Step into Finland's Kainuu Forest, and you'll notice traces of its animal inhabitants, from tracks in the soil to rustling leaves. This rarely trodden (by humans, at least) pan-continental taiga forest is a honeypot for European brown bears, which fish in the streams for sockeye salmon and forage among berry-spiked trees for winter fuel. Sightings are rare during the bears' hibernation period in the colder months, but there's a good chance of spotting one between spring and fall, when syrupy daylight hours are long and the animals more active and easy to find. Venture out in a canoe to spy them on the banks of the Lentua lake system, or hunker down in a hide to await the perfect close-up of Finland's "king of the forest."

" There's a good chance of spotting a bear between spring and fall, when syrupy daylight hours are long. "

▷ CARPATHIAN MOUNTAINS, ROMANIA

Play your part in shaping a new national park, where you can spot wolves, brown bears, and red deer from the comfort of your cabin.

Not everything in Bram Stoker's *Dracula* was far-fetched fiction. The Count may have been plucked from Romanian folklore, but the baying wolves were very real. They're still found in Transylvania today, flitting through the forests as flashes of gray and leaving clawed footprints in the snow as they hunt and howl their way across the Carpathian Mountains.

Cutting a sickle shape through Eastern Europe, the Carpathians curve southeast from the Czech Republic, through Slovakia, Poland, Hungary, the Ukraine and Romania, before petering out in northern Serbia. More than half of the range lies in Romania, in a wild mountainous region not of proper peaks—Moldoveanu, the highest, is barely half the size of Mont Blanc—but of exposed ridges, rippling hills, deep valleys and thick forests of ancient spruce and beech. As well as wolves, there are bears and lynxes here, too, in numbers so significant that together they make up the biggest European population of large carnivores.

This is the continent's last true wilderness, part of an ambitious rewilding project intent on turning central Romania into the "Yellowstone of Europe." Since 2009, philanthropists at the Foundation Conservation Carpathia have been buying up parcels of land across the Făgăraș Mountains in the Southern Carpathians, stitching them together into a nature reserve that they hope to hand over to the Romanian government one day, so it can be permanently protected in the form of a national park.

The reserve is accessible only as part of an organized overnight stay, at one of a pair of eco-friendly cabins set high up in the mountains. That this is a remote adventure

Eurasian Wolf

The most common subspecies of gray wolf found in Europe, the Eurasian wolf is comparatively slender, with a coarser coat that comes in shades of cream, gray, red, and black, or all of these colors combined.

Eurasian Lynx

The largest wildcats in Europe, Eurasian lynxes have a spotty, reddish-brown coat (which transforms into silvery-gray in winter) and a black-tipped bobtail. The tufts on their ears act as hearing aids.

is clear from the start: getting to the cabins involves driving off-road through the lush wilderness of the Dâmboviţa Valley, before continuing on foot when the track runs out. It's a steep but picturesque hike, skirting around lakes and passing through high meadow and pristine forest.

You'll arrive at your evening's base in time to watch the setting sun paint the treetops pink. The rustic cabins double up as cozy wildlife hides, and as dusk falls all eyes will turn to what's just outside the window: red deer, a wolverine, or maybe even a wolf or lynx. Many of the creatures here are more active at night, and you can stay up to look for them as long as you like, warmed by the heat of a wood-burning stove. Dawn brings with it pockets of early morning mist, hanging in the valley like strewn clumps of cotton wool, and the chance for more wildlife watching before breakfast. Then it's time to hike back out, stopping for a picnic before returning back down the trail to civilization.

One of two cabins in the Făgăraş Mountains in the Southern Carpathians

Wolverine

While they resemble small bears, wolverines are in fact the largest members of the weasel family. They have dark fur—broken by a lateral yellow stripe and a band above their eyes—and a thick bushy tail.

▷ BIAŁOWIEŻA FOREST, POLAND

Enter lowland Europe's last remaining primeval forest, and you'll be in with a chance of spotting the largest land mammal on the continent.

Long protected from logging activity, Poland's Białowieża Forest has become a safe haven for wildlife. Among its moss-draped, centuries-old trees, hundreds of rare birds and insects find shelter. Around them, red deer skitter through the glades in a blur of amber and fecund soils bloom with mushrooms the size of dinner plates. Look a little more carefully at the forest floor, though, and you'll find much bigger footprints here. Because this forest—a UNESCO Biosphere Reserve and World Heritage Site—is a vital refuge for European bison.

Hunted to near-extinction in the early 20th century, the bison were reintroduced here from captivity in the 1950s. They thrived in the forest's diverse environment, and today there are estimated to be around 500–900 individuals in Białowieża, together forming the largest herd in the world. The animals roam freely, so there's no science to anticipating their appearance; instead, sign up to a bison safari, carried out via vehicle or on foot. (Look for ethical tour operators that run only small-group tours and pledge to stay a respectful distance from the animals.) The expert guides know the areas in which the creatures are most likely to be spotted, and their noses are alert to even the slightest whiff of the herds. You'll also be able to visit the restricted parts of Białowieża only accessible in the company of a guide.

In winter, the huge beasts are a stirring sight, bracing against thick snowdrifts in their cold-weather coats; in summer, the solitary bulls join the herds for a boisterous breeding season that lasts until September. Whatever time of year you visit, it's hard to believe that this noble species was once on the brink of extinction—it makes seeing these resilient creatures feel like a rare privilege.

The Destined Dozen

European bison once roamed the continent from Russia to Spain but were steadily hunted to extinction. However, 12 individuals survived in zoological collections, and from these remaining animals, a breeding program was started. Their descendants were reintroduced to Europe's forests and flourished so greatly that there are now more than 6,000 living European bison in the world—every single one of them descended from those 12 individuals.

Far left Ancient woodland in Białowieża Forest
Left A bison herd in winter
Below A lone bison bull

Paragliding

Strapped in a harness, with heart racing, it feels insanely counterintuitive to run at top speed toward the edge of a cliff—but the second the wing-shaped parachute lifts you into the air, the feeling of weightlessness and the stunning bird's-eye view combine to create a surprisingly peaceful sensation. Paragliding in a tandem flight, with an instructor guiding you, requires no ability or experience on your part. It's so addictive, though, that you may be tempted to learn to fly solo. You just need to take that first leap of faith.

◁ GUDAURI, GEORGIA

Fly high above the soaring icy peaks and narrow folded valleys of the South Caucasus.

The stunning alpine landscapes of the South Caucasus have made Gudauri the leading ski resort in Georgia, but there's an even better way to experience these mountains: by soaring above the slopes in a paraglider. The landscape here is one of undulating, snow-dusted peaks and green and gold valleys cut through by snaking rivers. The scenery feels untamed, but that just adds to the beauty and the stillness that you feel during your flight. Taking off from the spectacular Jvari Pass, you'll enjoy views over the sheer-sided walls of Devil's Valley and then glide above the winding Georgian Military Highway. Carved through plunging gorges and precarious mountain passes, this historic road—still in use today—has carried merchants and invading hordes to Tbilisi, the country's capital, since antiquity.

◁ LAKE ANNECY, FRANCE

Soar peacefully above the cobalt blue of Lake Annecy, keeping an eye out for bearded vultures.

The mountainous limestone ridges that surround France's Lake Annecy, covered in a carpet of pine forest, make a spectacular backdrop for paragliding. They also shelter the serene valley in which the lake sits, meaning that the weather in these foothills remains reliably calm for flying (conditions in the nearby Alps, which rise impressively to the east, are often too volatile).

The forested hillsides of the Réserve Naturelle Marais du Bout, on the lake's southern edge, hide one of the most picturesque and popular spots from which to take off. From a grassy clearing in the trees, you'll charge down to the edge of the ridge until the wind fills out your parachute and carries you up into the ether. This tends to be the most heart-racing part of the whole experience; once your feet are off the ground and you're in the lap of the gods, you'll find yourself suspended in a state of stillness and quiet—at least until your instructor decides to start doing seesaws and spirals, that is.

While the sense of complete surrender to the elements is what makes paragliding thrilling, it's an illusion. Pilots use the conditions to their advantage, entering thermal vents (natural columns of warm and cool air) to gain and lose height, remaining in control throughout; the flight is no more dangerous than the car ride to the lake.

If you're really lucky, you'll have the chance to soar alongside a bearded vulture, reintroduced to the Alps in the 1980s. These red-eyed, golden-bodied creatures are magnificent, with a wingspan that can approach 10 ft (3 m); as they glide gracefully into the uplift of a thermal vent, your pilot will often follow them, raising your para-glider toward the heavens.

Beneath you, Lake Annecy is a constant presence. This bright-blue body of water slithers like a serpent between forested limestone ridges on either side, the sun glinting in numberless flashes like diamonds on its surface. Once you've taken it all in from up high, life on the ground might feel a little humdrum by comparison.

Paragliders rising up into the clear blue sky, with the waters of Lake Annecy below

Flying above the azure seas and white-sand beaches of Turkey's Turquoise Coast

△ ÖLÜDENIZ, TURKEY

Glide from a mighty mountain above the beaches and lagoons of Turkey's lush Turquoise Coast.

Forget the rugged valleys and soaring mountain peaks often associated with gliding hot spots: Ölüdeniz is something different. Instead of the usual alpine grandeur, you'll soar over lush Mediterranean landscapes, spurred on by a warm breeze. Happily, the area is blessed with a balmy climate, reliable weather, and fantastic thermals—all of which help make this Turkish seaside resort one of the best places in the world to paraglide.

From the towering summit of Mount Babadağ, just 3 miles (5 km) away from the sea, you'll drift toward the honey beaches and azure lagoons of the Turquoise Coast. Beneath the dome of cloudless sky, forested hills tumble down to meet the glittering waters of the Blue Lagoon and brilliant-white sands of Ölüdeniz Beach—the latter is the perfect place for a soft landing.

Coastal Foraging

Nothing could be further from the sterile fluorescent lights of the supermarket aisles than rummaging along a windswept coastline in search of your next meal. Summer seems the obvious season for foraging, but you'll be surprised by the generosity of nature's bounty, even in the colder months. The key is a little bit of preparation: check the tides and local bylaws, wear waterproof shoes, and, above all, eat only what you can safely identify.

◁ ARGYLL, SCOTLAND

Explore Argyll's pristine coastline in search of buried treasure: deliciously salty cockles hiding in the sand.

No stranger to large commercial seafood outfits, with a particular specialty in bivalves like mussels, cockles, and oysters, Argyll's crystal-clear waters and extensive coastline provide fertile ground for your own smaller-scale trawlings along the shore. You'll need to steer clear of the National Nature Reserve at Taynish and any Sites of Special Scientific Interest—important exceptions to the generous Scottish Outdoor Access Code that provides foragers with wide access to the land and coast—but that still leaves hundreds of miles of accessible seashore at your foraging fingertips.

There are few stretches of Argyll's coast that won't yield some treasure, but Ganavan, just north of Oban, is particularly well known for the abundance of common cockles buried in its intertidal zone. Time your visit to coincide with low tide, and embark on a bracing walk along the coast, wearing footwear sturdy enough to take on the task of plowing through damp sand and scrambling over limpet-covered rocks. Finding the cockles is relatively straightforward: simply look for small bulges in the sand, then plunge your fingers down and feel your way to your loot, adding to your bucket one small jewel at a time. From the main beach, it's a short walk along the coastal footpath to Little Ganavan—sometimes home to noisy otters, and almost always to more cockle-picking opportunities.

Top The tranquil strip of coastline at Ganavan Beach
Bottom left Searching for cockles
Bottom right Sautéed cockles served in their shells

Leave No Trace

Sustainability and responsibility are at the heart of the forager's code. Don't uproot plants from common land and pick only from populations where you can leave plenty behind—remember, wild plants are an important food source for local wildlife.

Looking over the County Galway coast from Connemara National Park

Spotter's Guide

Sea Radish

This common edible plant is found on sand and shingle. From June to August, it can be easily identified by its bright yellow flowers.

Channeled Wrack

This populous seaweed, with its distinctive curled fronds, grows around the high-water mark and is a familiar sight in County Galway.

Sea Beet

Also known as wild spinach, sea beet grows on shingle, between rocks, and among sand dunes, and is the ancient ancestor of beets and Swiss chard.

Sea Lettuce

Sea lettuce is found on the edge of rock pools and on rocks between the high- and low-water marks. Its green fronds have a rich umami flavor.

◁ GALWAY, IRELAND

With a smorgasbord of tasty sea plants, County Galway's coastline is a vegetarian forager's delight.

County Galway is home to some of Ireland's most striking scenery, and its rugged green landscape provides a tantalizing hint of the fertile pickings that can be found here. Although at first glance the coast might appear less promising than the verdant interior, look more closely and you'll find a huge variety of edible sea plants lying right at your feet.

As you stroll along the shoreline, the blustering wind at times invigorating, at others numbing, start by seeking out the vegetation set back from the sea. One of the easiest species to spot is sea radish, thanks to its rosette-shaped growth and yellow cruciform flowers. One bite leaves little wonder as to how this tough brassica got its name—the sharply serrated leaves are reminiscent of arugula but provide even more of a peppery kick. Another coastal favorite you're almost certain to spy is sea beet, clinging to the sand in bushes; it proliferates year-round, making it a valuable addition to the winter forager's arsenal. The sea beet's dark-green succulent leaves are pointed and shine glossily even on the dullest days and have an inky taste akin to spinach but with added depth.

Down by the water, in the stony shallows, keep your eyes open for fronds waving amid the roaring surf. Seaweeds such as sea lettuce and channeled wrack are woefully underused ingredients and are easily gathered from the battered rocks: simply snip the tops and leave the rest to regrow before moving on. Come evening, your earlier efforts will be richly rewarded with a variety of flavors and textures that shine with even the simplest preparation—perhaps eaten raw in a salad or lightly steamed as an accompaniment to seafood.

▽ OOSTERSCHELDE, NETHERLANDS

Bring a bucket and forage for shellfish in the seemingly endless expanse of the Oosterschelde.

Protected by the largest of the Netherlands' Delta Works (a series of constructions that protect parts of the country from the ravages of the sea), the tidal pools of the Oosterschelde sit amid an almost overwhelmingly flat landscape. On a calm day, the movement of the surrounding water is a gentle lull; during a squall, it's violent and terrifying.

Yet it is in these capricious coastal ecosystems that you'll discover the beach forager's delight: mussels, oysters, and periwinkles peeping from rocks, dotted across the Oosterschelde in tidal pools and oyster beds that are largely only accessible on foot. The flow of seawater enables the shellfish populations here to thrive, providing a feast of the freshest produce money didn't even buy.

Dozens of oysters exposed by the low tide in an oyster bank at Oosterschelde

Scaling an arched
cliff next to the sea
in Sicily

Climbing

Traditionally the preserve of mavericks and adventurers, climbing is very much an activity with its roots in the world's wildest places. There are different ways to approach it—either as sport climbing, with harnesses and ropes on predefined routes, or traditional ("trad") climbing, where you place your own equipment as you ascend—but whichever you choose, one thing's for sure: you'll need a big dose of bravery and a head for heights.

◁ SICILY, ITALY

An established winter climbing destination, Sicily offers a huge variety of ascents in a beautiful island setting.

Enveloped by the Mediterranean at the foot of Italy, Sicily is a postcard-perfect island of volcanic peaks, idyllic beaches, historic towns, and ancient sites. It's a popular destination with sunseekers in summer, but climbers know that there's an even better season to visit—winter. Not only is the island much quieter at this time of year, but the mild temperatures make for blissful climbing conditions.

The scene here is focused on the northern and eastern coasts, in particular the areas around San Vito Lo Capo, Palmero, Messina, and Siracusa. Surface-wise, you'll find mainly limestone rock, but in all other aspects, you'll have almost endless options—sport or trad, single pitch (climbed in one go) or multi pitch (climbed in stages), and mountains, caves, or sea cliffs. There's enough to keep you going all the way through till spring.

▷ FRANKENJURA, GERMANY

Hone your skills at this world-class sport-climbing
destination, with thousands of routes to practice on.

Frankenjura, a rural area located between the cities of
Nürnberg, Bamberg, and Bayreuth in Bavaria, is a sport
climber's paradise. That's no exaggeration—with over 10,000
routes at 1,000 sites, there truly is a climb here for every level,
from eager beginners to those looking to push the grades.

That's as long as you like climbing on limestone, of
course. Different rock types provide different climbing
experiences, and the limestone crags at Frankenjura are
commonly peppered with indents and pockets that take
only one or two fingers—it's a real test of how strong your
digits are. Vertical and overhanging walls are the norm,
so the focus tends to be on more powerful climbing over
shorter distances; most routes are single pitch, with heights
ranging between 33 ft (10 m) and 131 ft (40 m).

Encompassing a large area of thick forest, Frankenjura
not only has routes for climbers of every aptitude, but it
also has crags for every weather condition. Some are found
in the shade of trees, enabling you to climb comfortably in
the heat of high summer, while others in open, sunny spots
dry quickly after wet weather, so you're not forced to hang
around waiting after a rain shower. And if the elements ever
get too extreme, there's always a backup—Frankenjura is
known for its high density of traditional breweries and
climber-endorsed coffee-and-cake shops.

With so much choice, it can be tricky to know where
to start. The crags closest to campsites are the most busy,
so just head a little deeper into the forest and you'll soon
find a secluded spot. Routes range from 1 (novice) to 9c
(high-level elite); easier options can be found on crags
such as Schlosszwergwand and Maximilianswand, while
experienced climbers will want to head for Action Directe.
The world's first 9a graded route, it was redpointed
(successfully free-climbed) by sports-climbing superstar
Wolfgang Güllich in 1991 and has lured the best of the best
ever since. If you're not wedded to bagging a set route,
then branch out—there are 10,000 to choose from, after all.

Redpoint Pioneer

Frankenjura is the birthplace of the climbing
term "redpoint." It was invented in 1975 by
German climber Kurt Albert, to describe when
a route had been free-climbed—scaled from
bottom to top without the aid of safety
equipment but with protection in place in
case of a fall. (This is different to free soloing,
which involves climbing without a harness or
any protection.) Each time Kurt successfully
completed a route, he would mark it with a red
dot to show it could be climbed without aids.

Top Tying a knot in
preparation for a climb
Above A harness stocked
with quickdraw clips
Left Making a technically
challenging ascent

Climbing on granite in the High Tatras, on the border between Poland and Slovakia

△ TATRA MOUNTAINS, POLAND

Venture into the wilderness of the Tatra Mountains for a climbing experience with an off-grid feel.

The Tatra Mountains stand proudly between Poland and Slovakia and are the smallest alpine range in Europe. They're proof, if it was needed, that bigger doesn't always mean better. This untamed, rocky region is a UNESCO Biosphere Reserve, rich with an incredible diversity of flora and fauna. High granite crags tower above dense pine forest, creating a climbing experience that feels wild and remote. There are routes on both sides of the border, but it's the ones in Poland, in the High Tatras, that are most easily accessible. These may not be the epic rock faces of the Alps, but you'll be enjoying the back-to-nature vibe so much that you won't really care.

Leave No Trace

There are strict rules to protect the environment of the Tatra Mountains, which mean you can climb only in designated areas and have to log your climbing plans in books found in mountain shelters. You must also stay on the designated walking paths unless with a registered guide.

▷ PAKLENICA NATIONAL PARK, CROATIA

Scale the big walls of the Velika Paklenica gorge, amid a stunning national park.

Located by the Adriatic Sea, Paklenica National Park encompasses a wild area of thick forest set against the rugged backdrop of the Velebit mountain range. The karst landscape here is rumpled by the creases of millennia-old rock formations, rising and falling in an alternating pattern of peaks and canyons. It's the latter that are of interest to climbers here, particularly the Velika Paklenica gorge—its steep cliffs are crisscrossed by an established network of around 600 climbing routes.

Many of the routes are found in Klanci, the narrowest part of the gorge, which is close to the park entrance. The climbs here are generally single pitch and welcoming for visitors of all abilities, with the easy accessibility making it a good option for families. But it's the big wall climbing of the Anića Kuk rock face, a little deeper into the canyon, that really gets people excited. The highest point in the area, this 1,148 ft (350 m) crag is a formidable slab of near-vertical rock and has more than 100 routes of varying grades available. Scaling its giddy heights brings well-earned views out over the park and the Adriatic, including a striking bird's-eye perspective of the narrow canyon and its winding ribbon of river.

Navigating a difficult rock face in the scenic Velika Paklenica gorge

The dancing green bands of the
aurora borealis flickering over
the Arctic city of Trømso

Northern Lights

Made up of intense red, purple, blue or (most commonly) green swirls, the aurora borealis electrifies night skies at higher latitudes. While usually appearing to the naked eye as only a ghostly white with hints of color, add in a camera and its true beauty emerges. A sense of awe comes from watching these dancing celestial veils, as does gratitude—after all, displays are never guaranteed, regardless of how much you spend, appeal to deities, or endure subzero temperatures.

◁ TROMSØ, NORWAY

Venture deep into the Arctic Circle to glimpse the shimmering "green lady" dancing above Norway's ice-enshrouded landscapes.

Once a hangout for hardy polar explorers such as Fridtjof Nansen, Umberto Nobile and the world-renowned Roald Amundsen, Tromsø is known as the gateway to the high Arctic. The city, which blankets the ruggedly beautiful island of Tromsøya, is nestled amid a wild panorama of endless skies; snowcapped jagged peaks; and icy, steel-blue water. But it's neither the city's adventurous history nor its fjord-meets-mountain setting that lures most visitors this far north—it's the chance to see the multi-colored glimmering and twisting shapes of the ethereal northern lights.

These flickering veils—affectionately called the "green lady" by locals—regularly appear in the skies near Tromsø. This is largely thanks to location; the city lies right at the top of Norway and is well within the Arctic Circle due to its position on the 69th parallel. This close to the North Pole, the magnetic activity that allows the aurora to bloom is much stronger than it is farther south. The long nights of the Arctic winter, which lasts from October to March, also help, providing the inky black skies needed for the aurora to really shine. ▶

Strands of light swirling over
Norway's frosted landscape

∧

Insider Tip

Finding the northern lights is
an art and a science, so don't
be tempted by a DIY chase.
Instead, head out with a local
guide. They use a network of
experienced contacts who
share live information with
each other about the behavior
and location of the sometimes
elusive lights.

While it's sometimes possible to spy the lights from
the city itself, the best displays are found well away from
any light pollution. As a result, each night, small convoys
of aurora hunters—led by experienced guides—flee Tromsø
by 4WD and snowmobile. Crossing over to the mainland via
a striking bridge that spans the deep-blue Malangen fjord,
these determined explorers head deep into the snow-clad
interior. Providing the skies are clear of clouds and there's
little moonlight, the chance of seeing the northern lights is
high—although their intensity can vary due to the amount
of solar activity.

The conditions, of course, do not always play ball,
and the tenacious guides have been known to cross the

Above Preparing to
go in search of the
northern lights
on snowmobiles
Right Admiring the
pale green veils of
the aurora borealis

*"It's easy to see why the Vikings
believed the lights to be a bridge
to Asgard, the land of the gods. "*

border into Finland in their efforts to find good enough
weather for a sighting. To be in with the best chance of
getting the full celestial experience, then, it's definitely
worth dedicating at least a couple of nights to chasing
the aurora.

When, at last, you spy them, these swirling strands will
steal the breath from your lungs. Some nights they can be
a modest band of pale light drifting gently across the sky,
while on others they're a multitude of individually colored
curtains that dance, flare, flicker, and spiral into a single
fantastical scene. Watching their transcendental dance,
it's easy to see why the Vikings believed the lights to be a
bridge to Asgard, the land of the gods.

The Science Behind the Lights

The origins of the aurora begin deep in space,
when the sun produces solar winds—made up
of electrically charged particles—that then drift
toward the Earth. While most bounce off the
planet's magnetic field, some manage to sneak
through, and are channeled down toward the
North and South poles. When these charged
particles collide with the upper atmosphere,
they release energy, creating dancing rings of
light around both of the Earth's magnetic
poles. In the Northern Hemisphere, this is
called the aurora borealis or northern lights.

SAARISELKÄ, FINLAND

Regular aurora displays mean you can kick back and relax at this pretty resort-village.

Nestled well within the Auroral Oval—a ring encircling the magnetic north pole where auroral activity is high—the area around Saariselkä is treated to up to 200 northern lights displays a year. While a number of "aurora chases" set out to hunt for the lights each night, you don't need to go far from the village—or even leave the comfort of your own bed—to see these otherworldly bands of glimmering light. Dotted around the edge of Saariselkä are a number of wooden and igloo-inspired cabins, whose glass roofs let you admire the aurora from the cozy warmth of the indoors. Wrap yourself up in a blanket, grab a hot chocolate, and watch as the shimmering veils perform above you.

Top left The northern lights dancing above the glass igloos of Kakslauttanen Arctic Resort, close to Saariselkä

JÖKULSÁRLÓN, ICELAND

Admire the aurora borealis twice over at this iceberg-filled lagoon.

Sitting in the shadow of Vatnajökull, Europe's largest glacier, this UNESCO-protected lagoon in southern Iceland is filled with glasslike icebergs drifting ethereally over calm waters. This unearthly scene is made even more spectacular between October and March, with the arrival of the dancing northern lights. Lighting up the sky above, these flickering, multicolored strands—clearly seen thanks to the lack of light pollution—are reflected in the lagoon's tranquil, mirrorlike waters, and glint and gleam off the shining spearmint-colored icebergs. The overall result is dazzling, making you feel as though the aurora's shimmering veils are drifting up from the sea as well as down from the sky.

Bottom left Bands of light glimmering over the iceberg-filled waters of Jökulsárlón lagoon

MORAY COAST, SCOTLAND

Swap Scandinavia for this craggy coastal spot in the Scottish Highlands.

Parts of northern Scotland share the same latitude as Norway, making it a reliable bet for sightings of the "Mirrie Dancers"—as the aurora is known locally—in winter. Particularly good odds are offered by the Moray area's coastline between Brodie and Cullen, which gazes northward into the sea, free of obstruction from land or the blinding lights of cities. For the best chance of a sighting, find a rural spot—such as the moorland alongside the A940 road above Forres, the secluded Clashach Cove, or near the medieval ruins of Duffus Castle—and watch the lights as they skitter across the night sky. It'll be freezing, but fear not—a dram of local single malt will keep you warm as you watch.

Top right Flares of emerald- and lemon-colored light illuminating the night sky over Scotland's Moray Coast

ABISKO, SWEDEN

Statistically, nowhere gives lights-seekers a better chance than this village in Lapland.

The "Blue Hole"—that's the nickname for the unique microclimate that makes the village of Abisko such a hot spot for the aurora borealis. Found 150 miles (240 km) inside the Arctic Circle amid Swedish Lapland, the diminutive settlement is enclosed by a mountainous ring that seems to block clouds or rain—clear skies being critical to *norrsken* (northern lights) appearances, along with the absence of light pollution. As such, keen-eyed visitors staying here for three days or longer are estimated to have an astounding 88 percent chance of witnessing some stunning celestial cinema taking place above the ice-blanketed Arctic landscape.

Bottom right The almost fluorescent aurora borealis hanging above a snowy landscape near Abisko in Sweden

Forest Bathing

Forest bathing is an English translation of the Japanese phrase *Shinrin-yoku*, which is the simple act of spending quiet, mindful time in nature—especially forests and woodlands—in order to support your whole mind and body well-being. Centered around noticing nature, and calmly and deeply breathing the forest air, this respectful and sustainable practice has been scientifically proven to improve everything from your immune system to your mood. To feel the benefits of healing time among the trees, simply turn off your phone, slow down your pace, and open all your senses to the natural world around you.

Looking skyward toward the treetops in Belarus's ancient Belovezhskaya Pushcha

◁ BELOVEZHSKAYA PUSHCHA, BELARUS

Take it slow on a dark, damp, and sun-dappled wander through Europe's oldest primeval forest.

Straddling substantial swathes of western Belarus and eastern Poland, Belovezhskaya Pushcha is one of the largest and last remnants of an ancient forest. Born after the last Ice Age approximately 10,000 years ago, this mixed woodland once covered northeastern Europe like a dark, wet blanket.

Given the size of the forest, bathing here is best experienced over a minimum of two days. This will give you ample time to move slowly and thoughtfully, keeping your eyes open for an astounding array of flora and fauna, whether that's tiny fungi, rare beetles, or nearly lost species such as European wolf and lynx. As you wander, breath in the damp, earthy scent of the trees, whose branches creak and groan in the wind, and gaze at the shafts of golden light that filter through the forest's dark overstory.

The highlight here is a number of notably tall, ancient oak trees, whose crooked, wizened branches spiral out from portly trunks. Trace a path toward these characterful trees, which have been given names such as Great Mamamuszi, The King of Nieznanowo, and Patriarch Oak (pick up a map from the visitor center). Try to encircle your arms around the rough trunks of these giants, whose gnarled forms have stood in the forest for around 500 years.

Walking through a
deep-green pine forest
in Lithuania

△ SIGHTSEEING FOREST PATH, MARCINKONYS, LITHUANIA

Immerse yourself in the sights and smells of
a pine forest on this short trail.

Blanketed with deep-green forest, shimmering lakes, and
snaking rivers, Lithuania is a country of stunning natural
beauty. Delve into it by wandering along one of many
national, government-designated "Cognitive Paths" (nature
trails); these routes, by wending their way through some
of the country's most nature-rich spots, encourage
visitors to take time to connect with the natural world.

One of the best paths is found among the lush, river-
webbed landscapes of Dzukija National Park in southern
Lithuania. Known as the Sightseeing Forest Path, this flat
trail takes you on a 2.2-mile (3.6 km) loop through the pine-
wood groves of Marcinkonys village. Here, straight-trunked
pines rise elegantly toward the blue sky, their swaying
branches creating dancing sunbeams. Beneath these
stately trees, mushrooms—including gold-hued chan-
terelles and coral-like morel—sprout determinedly across
the soft green forest floor. The trail might be short, but
there's plenty to make you linger, including the sweet
smell of the pines that permeates the air all around.

▷ SONIAN FOREST, BELGIUM

An accessible meander through ancient beech
forest just a stone's-throw from Brussels.

Sonian Forest—a UNESCO World Heritage Site known
locally as the "Beech Cathedral"—is famed for its evenly
spread, dense, and ancient beech stands that date back
to the last Ice Age. This woodland is the largest existing
remnant of the Iron-Age "Charcoal Forest" (so named
because of the eventual fate of these old trees as fuel)
that once reached all the way to northern France.
Located just 30 minutes by bus from the center of
Brussels, it is a remarkably accessible place to soak
up the peace of the trees, with wide trails that are
solid under both foot and wheelchair.

Wandering along the gently winding paths, you might
spy deer, red fox, or—if you're lucky—one of Sonian's 14
species of bats (five of which are protected), which nest
in the hollows and crevices of the trunks and branches.
Dotted throughout the forest are a number of lakes, whose
tranquil banks offer the opportunity to pause and reflect;
sitting by the water, drift into a meditative calm as you
listen to the gentle rustling of nearby beech trees. Forest
bathing has pedigree here, with the woodland once housing a monastery, convent and cloister for praying monks
and nuns. By slowing down and absorbing the oxygen-
rich air in Brussels' "Wild Lung," you are joining in a rich
contemplative tradition dating back to the early 1200s.

" *Sitting by the water, drift into a*
meditative calm as you listen to the
gentle rustling of nearby beech trees. "

Rewilding the Forest

Over time, Sonian Forest has been divided by roads and railroad lines into different pockets of woodland. This habitat fragmentation has led to a decline in wildlife for many reasons, including increasing competition among species. However, thanks to the efforts of the European Rewilding Network, "wildlife corridors" are being created to connect these separated habitats, allowing animals such as roe deer, European beaver, and wild boar to roam freely through the whole forest again.

Wandering through a rust-red carpet of beech leaves in Belgium's Sonian Forest

Scuba
Diving

A kaleidoscope of life, as endlessly diverse and fascinating as that on dry land, awaits those who venture beneath the waves on a scuba-diving trip. With the aid of an air tank, mask, and flippers, you can explore parts of the planet long out of reach for humans, enjoying a 360-degree view of the underwater world. Whether in the Arctic Circle or the Mediterranean, in the hulks of old shipwrecks or volcanic ravines in rift valley lakes, scuba diving promises to unlock untold natural mysteries.

Examining the Christ the Abyss statue by Guido Galletti in Portofino Marine Park

◁ PORTOFINO MARINE PARK, ITALY

Plunge into the waters of Portofino Marine Park, where nature has reclaimed man-made objects to create an underwater playground.

Located in the most northerly reaches of the Italian Mediterranean, Portofino Marine Park forms a broad arc around Mount Portofino, which juts out into the sea from the mainland. A rich ecosystem flourishes in the park's subterranean caves and open water, but humans have left their mark here, too. One of the most eye-catching relics is a 8 ft (2.5 m) underwater statue of Christ the Abyss, standing with mottled bronze arms raised upward to the heavens. Created by Italian sculptor Guido Galletti, it stands as a monument to those who lost their lives at sea—a reality borne out by the shipwrecks that fleck the seabed here.

Several of these sunken boats, such as *Genova*, *Haven*, and *Bolzaneto*, have become some of the area's best-known dive sites. Their coral-covered remains are a haven for marine life, with diverse species—from grumpy-looking groupers to perfectly camouflaged scorpion fish—awaiting discovery amid their murky ruins.

Right Diving through Iceland's Silfra fissure, between two tectonic plates
Bottom left Admiring the view over Thingvallavatn Lake
Bottom right The crystal-clear waters of Silfra, composed of filtered glacial meltwater

▷ SILFRA, ICELAND

Dive down into the icy depths of this fissure to swim between two tectonic plates, home to "troll hair" algae and some of the world's clearest water.

Iceland is no stranger to singular natural phenomena—from black-sand beaches to the midnight sun—but perhaps its most spectacular example is this volcanic rift beneath an ice-blue glacial lake. The Silfra fissure, on the rim of Thingvallavatn Lake, was formed in 1789 by the drifting of the Eurasian and North American tectonic plates, which creep an inch farther apart every year. This builds tension, which erupts in earthquakes once every decade, wreaking more creative destruction and reshaping Iceland's beautiful volcanic landscapes anew.

The chance to scuba dive here is not to be missed. The first thing you'll notice when you plunge into the fissure is how shockingly cold the water is. At just above freezing for most of the year, around 36–39°F (2–4°C), it's sure to take your breath away—and not just for the beauty that lies beneath. Even with the insulating benefits of a dry suit, you can count on some numb fingers and toes afterward. Very quickly, though, any thoughts of the cold evaporate as you submerge yourself into the fissure and take in an alien underwater world through the prism of some of the clearest water on the planet.

Silfra's water was left behind by the Langjökull glacier, which has now retreated to around 20 miles (32 km) north-east of the lake. Glacial meltwater is pure already, but here it is doubly so, thanks to an eruption of the Skjaldbreiður volcano around 12,000 years ago. The porous lava fields that were created by the eruption formed an aquifer, a natural underground water purifier. The water that you're diving in has been passing through this filter for anything from 30 to 100 years—it's good enough to drink and has visibility of up to 328 ft (100 m), ranking among the purest in the world.

Rainbows on the Rocks

In certain weather conditions, the waters of Silfra are illuminated with a beautiful natural phenomenon, whereby the sun shines through the water and casts rainbows on the rocks and lake bed. This is thanks to Silfra's water being quite literally crystal clear—it refracts light in the same way that a diamond would do.

The focal point of the dive is a swim through the so-called Big Crack, where it's narrow enough in places to touch both sides of the rift, and therefore two continents, at once—the only place on Earth this is possible. But it's the heavenly Silfra Cathedral that's the most awe-inspiring section of the fissure, with its plunging cavern walls stretching to 328 ft (100 m) long and 66 ft (20 m) deep.

The scenery in Silfra is beautifully desolate, but it's by no means devoid of life. The rocks are covered in neon-green Tetraspora and Klebsormidium algae. The latter is known as "troll hair," and it's easy to see why as its unruly tendrils float off into the water. Look carefully, and you might also spot the gunmetal flash or pink underbelly of an Arctic char among the algae's green fingers. And thanks to the crystal-clear water, you can admire it all in glorious high definition.

Swimming through the
ethereal waters of the Blue
Hole in Gozo

▷ GOZO, MALTA

Plumb the depths of Gozo's Blue Hole, a unique
subaqueous geological formation.

With its perfect round "O" of azure water, Gozo's aptly
named Blue Hole—a collapsed underwater limestone
cave—is one of the most picturesque dive sites in the
Mediterranean. A dive here begins much like any other:
as you slip beneath the surface, the warm colors and
bright lights recede, replaced by the murky gloom and
echoey amplified sounds of the underwater world. Glance
up, though, and you'll catch the startling sight of an
impossibly blue shaft of light penetrating the shadows
of the sinkhole, framed by the walls of the former cave.

From above, it looks like the Blue Hole stands separate
from the sea, divided by a wall of coralline limestone, but
as you dive deeper, a connecting passageway reveals
itself. Beyond here lies open water and the Coral Gardens,
where abundant sea life—including kaleidoscopic wrasses,
jellyfish, and damselfish—lurks between the rocky
plateaus and canyons surrounding you.

Nearby are the sunken remains of the Azure Window,
a natural arch that used to sit next to the Blue Hole. The
inevitable collapse of this former landmark was mourned
by many, but what was lost to the land has been claimed
by the deep. The sight of its sharp fragments poking up
from the seabed provides a poignant reminder of the
delicate natural balance that underpins this beautiful
oceanic landscape.

The Collapse of the Azure Window

The Azure Window, known in Maltese as the
it-Tieqa tad-Dwejra (Dwejra Window), was one
of the island's biggest attractions prior to its
collapse in March 2017. Thought to have itself
been created by the collapse of a sea cave in the
19th century, the formation suffered from
natural erosion exacerbated by thousands of
visitors in the 1990s and 2000s, before it fell
completely during a heavy storm.

Leave No Trace

If you opt to dive without a
wet suit, wear a reef-friendly
sunscreen that does not
contain oxybenzone and
octinoxate, two chemicals
known to cause coral
bleaching, which can cause
corals to die.

▽ CHIOS, GREECE

Little known beyond local circles, Chios harbors
an eclectic array of spectacular dive sites.

With its paradisaical setting amid the turquoise waters of
the Aegean Sea, it's difficult to believe that Chios attracts
few travelers from outside of Greece. It is, after all, the
country's fifth-largest island. But others' loss is your gain,
as you'll have the diverse dive sites here almost all to
yourself. And there are plenty of appealing options to
choose from—mysterious underwater caverns, colorful
coral reefs, haunting shipwrecks, and sheer sea walls that
teem with marine life. Follow darting shoals of perches,
wrasses, and tunnies, and keep an eye out for the huge
tuna and swordfish that sometimes stray into these waters.
If you time your visit for the summer months, you may even
be lucky enough to spy turtles.

Above Looking toward the shore of Chios
while on a dive in the Aegean Sea

Trail

Running

The idea of trail running seems simple—it's running, just not on roads. But this fails to describe the sheer variety it offers. You'll stride out on rocky mountain paths, along shady forest tracks, over muddy fells, and across sandy beaches. Trail running is wonderfully tactile, too—your feet really feel the ground, connecting fully with the landscapes you traverse, reading the contour lines with your legs. With reasonable fitness and the right gear, the continent is yours to explore.

◁ DOLOMITES, ITALY

Lope around this lofty region of limestone peaks for epic Alpine views and a mix of Italian and Austrian culture.

Whether your first sight of the Dolomites inspires wonder or worry depends largely on whether the sun's out. When they gleam white beneath azure skies on a summer's day, these limestone massifs just might be Europe's most beautiful mountains. When lowering clouds mask the blue, they loom like broken teeth, stark and forbidding. But whatever the weather, they demand a closer look. The best way to do that is on two legs, running the varied trails that lace high plateaus, wildflower meadows, and verdant valleys.

The excellent infrastructure set up to serve skiers is a boon for runners in summer. Well-marked trails and cable cars provide easy access to the high plains and peaks, and a generous scattering of mountain huts serve surprisingly gourmet fare to hungry runners. This southern patch of the Alps has more than a whiff of Austria about it, not least in the dark-wood cabins that stud the hillsides and the language spoken in many regions. But it's definitely Italian, too. You'll fuel up on both linguine and apple strudel, on ravioli and *kaiserschmarrn* (shredded pancakes with cream).

Crucially, it's gorgeous, with an enormous diversity of trails. You can run all the way up the Dolomites' highest peak, Marmolada (10,965 ft/3,342 m), or over the undulating plateau of Pralongià. You'll pass World War I trenches etched into mountainsides and be whistled at by cheeky marmots as chamois bound nearby and choughs wheel above. Even better, each run ends with the knowledge that there are more spectacular trails to try tomorrow.

Top Heading over a high plateau in the Dolomites
Bottom left Dining on tasty *kaiserschmarrn*
Bottom right Running along a rocky mountain path

▷ DINARIC ALPS, BOSNIA AND HERZEGOVINA

Known for their spectacular limestone rock formations, the undiscovered mountains of the Dinaric Alps offer a true explorer experience for expert trail runners.

Stretching through the Balkans from Albania to Slovenia, the Dinaric Alps offer experienced trail runners the chance to bound along craggy mountain paths in glorious solitude. Thanks to less-developed trails and limited tourism infrastructure, these mountains are far quieter—and much wilder— than their more famous siblings, the Western Alps, to the east.

Here, you can take your pick of quiet trails: some lead you up through rich Mediterranean-style grasslands to sunlit peaks reaching over 6,560 ft (2,000 m), others into remote highland communities that have existed for centuries. Yet more lead you deep into forested valleys—dotted with life-giving fresh springs—that remain relatively pristine and bio-diverse; as you run, you might see the prints of both brown bears and wolves, who still live wild in these parts.

As you fly along the trails, you'll never be far from the scent of dwarf pine drifting on warm updraughts of air, or from the sight of some spectacular rock formation. The Bosnian Mountains offer a unique limestone geology that will appeal to rock lovers; here lies a landscape of caves, canyons and moonlike plateaus, as well as the world's largest karstic limestone field.

Start your self-crafted "runventure" in the east of Bosnia and you can tackle the trails that lead you to the nation's highest peak, Maglic, with the option of crossing the soft border into Montenegro for tea in a hut by the heart-shaped Trnovacko Lake. Alternatively, pack light for a leave-no-trace overnighter and run the single-track high valley path along Rakitinica Canyon to Lukomir village for a taste of traditional Bosnian highland life. Wherever you go, you'll be part of a select group of adventurous runners who have explored these remote mountains.

A group running through the remote mountains of the Dinaric Alps in the fall

△ LOCH AN EILEIN, SCOTLAND

This gentle, flowing trail captures everything that wild Scotland has to offer in microcosm.

Crumbling castles and tangled forests, tranquil lakes and soaring, moody mountains—you'll find all of these quintessentially Scottish sights on this run in the heart of the Cairngorms National Park. Looping around tiny Loch an Eilein, the flat 3-mile (5 km) trail follows shoreside paths lined by towering Scots pine, their branches home to rust-hued red squirrels and diminutive crested tits—both iconic Scottish species. As you weave your way around the lake, steal glimpses of the ever-looming Cairngorm Mountains through the gaps in the trees and spy the lake's small island, on which sit the overgrown ruins of a 14th-century castle. The run might be a short one, but all along the route, side trails lead off in different directions, enticing you to journey even deeper into the stunning, untamed Scottish wilderness.

Above Looking over the tranquil waters of forest-fringed Loch an Eilein, the rounded peaks of the Cairngorms looming in the background

⌃ Explore More

Just over 5 miles (8 km) away from Loch an Eilein is picturesque Loch Morlich, known for its sandy beach. Laze on the soft golden sands here or try kayaking, canoeing, or stand-up paddleboarding on the lake's calm waters.

Road Cycling

Road cycling encompasses pedaling on any kind of paved surface, from smooth bike paths to bone-rattling cobblestone lanes to zigzagging mountain roads. Blending physical challenge with a feeling of immersion in the landscape, this two-wheeled activity offers a wonderful sense of freedom. It doesn't matter whether you ride a sleek racer, a handcycle, or a tandem tourer—the roads are calling.

Rolling along flat roads through the Netherlands' lush windmill-dotted countryside

◁ AMSTERDAM TO UTRECHT, NETHERLANDS

Pedal through peaceful meadows and along canal paths on this idyllic route from Amsterdam to Utrecht.

The Netherlands has 22,990 miles (37,000 km) of glorious cycling paths to choose from. But if you're looking for one that weaves together everything that's special about the Dutch countryside, try the 25-mile (40 km) ride from the capital to the medieval city of Utrecht.

Rolling along gloriously flat terrain, you'll glide through bucolic countryside and stroll alongside canals, looking up at windmills and passing by flower-dotted meadows. Cyclists in the Netherlands have absolute right of way, so even going in and out of towns, you and your bike rule the roads.

Yes, you could cycle this in half a day—many of the lycra-clad *wielrenners* (sports cyclists) zooming past do so—but this leisurely route invites an idle pace: picnic canalside, before ending in Utrecht with a restorative glass of *jenever*.

◁ CURONIAN SPIT, LITHUANIA

This enchanting peninsula is ideal for cyclists who want big views for moderate pedal power.

Inhale the fragrant sea breeze as you roll along the largely flat seaside paths of the Curonian Spit, a UNESCO-protected sliver of land stretching from Lithuania to Russia's Kaliningrad region. The EuroVelo 10 cycling path extends along the whole peninsula, meaning you'll get to enjoy great signage and well-maintained trails as you go.

While you could pedal the full length of the spit, the 39-mile (63 km) Lithuanian section is perfect for a day trip. Starting in Smiltynė in the fresh glow of morning, you'll cycle the day away, passing by pillowy golden sand dunes, ghostly forests of silver-barked birch trees and colorful beach towns like Juodkrantė. At last, you'll reach the sleepy town of Nida. Its oceanside boardwalk allows you to drink in views of the Curonian Bay from your saddle as the setting sun drenches it in amber light.

Left Aerial view of the Curonian Spit at sunset
Above Cycling along a forested section of the route

Left Riding along
the winding hairpins
of Sa Calobra
Right A group
of cyclists rolling
through Mallorca

◁ MALLORCA, SPAIN

Pro cyclists and amateurs alike flock to this Balearic island for sensational road biking year-round.

If Mallorca is legendary in road-cycling circles, then its Serra de Tramuntana is the promised land. The backbone of northwest Mallorca, this impressive ridge of mountains and its snaking, switchback roads entice lycra-clad cyclists in all seasons—though spring, before temperatures soar, is most popular with those in the know. Classic touring roads here include the Col de Sóller, celebrated for its lack of traffic (cars take a tunnel through the mountain); Sa Calobra, much loved for those roller-coaster hairpins; and Cap de Formentor, a sensational ascent through jagged limestone rock to the end of the peninsula. All of these smooth mountain roads—dotted with scenic viewpoints known as miradors in Spanish—sweep through gloriously rugged terrain that plummets steeply to the sea.

" This impressive ridge of mountains and its snaking, switchback roads entice lycra-clad cyclists in all seasons. "

▽ CIRO TRAIL, BOSNIA AND HERZEGOVINA

Following an old railroad line, this trail is an open-air museum dedicated to the area's recent past.

The Ciro Trail traces the tracks of the narrow-gauge railroad that once connected Mostar in Bosnia and Herzegovina with Dubrovnik in Croatia. Starting in either Ivanica or Trebinje, this 87-mile (140 km) cycle path runs to Mostar through a picturesque rural region that was badly affected by the Balkans War in the 1990s. As you pedal along the mostly paved route—following disused tracks over bridges and through tunnels—you'll pass by evidence of the conflict, including abandoned villages, crumbling stations, and signs warning of landmines just off the trail. Upon your arrival into Mostar, still dotted with the ruins of bombed buildings, the region's troubled history hits home—but so does the possibility of its regeneration, seen in its beautifully restored Old Town, and bustling pubs and restaurants, filled with fellow cyclists.

The historic riverside city of Mostar, the final stop on the Ciro Trail

▷ BEARA PENINSULA, IRELAND

Escape the crowds on this loop through one of
western Ireland's most dramatic and yet least-
visited landscapes.

The Beara Peninsula may not have the name recognition of
its more famous Irish cousins (think Dingle and the Ring of
Kerry), but don't let its low profile fool you—this is one of
the best places to go road cycling in Europe. Beara's roads
are too narrow and tortuous for big tour buses to ply, so—
despite the region's dramatic landscape, abundance of
historical sights, enchanting fairy legends, and flourishing
food scene—you'll be able to ride here without seeing
more than a handful of tourists.

The best way to explore Beara by bike is on the Beara
Way Cycling Route. Sticking to mostly country roads and
keeping close to the coast, this trail loops for 86 miles
(138 km) around the wild and rugged peninsula, passing
through colorful towns and villages along the way. Happily,
you've got the freedom to join the road wherever you
choose, as the route has no official start or end point.

The riding along the Beara Way ranges from relatively flat,
like the stretch from Adrigole to Castletownbere, to gut-
bustingly steep, like the hills that encircle the tiny artists'
haven of Allihies. The hardest grades are usually short, but
beginners should make sure they have a few good climbs
under their belts before venturing here. Because the Beara
is so compact, it's possible for ambitious riders to traverse
the entire peninsula in a single, epic day. But every nook
deserves exploring—from the alpine splendor of Glanmore
Lake to the end-of-the-world solitude of Dursey Island,
both of which are short detours off the main route. The
villages (and pubs) are rarely more than 19 miles (30 km)

apart, and excellent B&Bs, hostels ,and campsites abound,
making the peninsula perfect to try your hand at touring
or to explore with a series of day rides.

One of the prettiest sections of the route runs from the
wooded village of Glengarriff to Adrigole. From here, as you
roll past rocky hills and through open meadows, you may spot
the magenta tufts of Irish marsh orchids and hear the screech
of a rare white-tailed sea eagle. You'll be warmed up by the
time you hit Adrigole, a tiny village that sits beneath the
glacier-scoured rock of Hungry Hill. Here, the route continues
west alongside Bantry Bay, but if you have the time, take a
detour up Healy Pass—this road weaves around the dramatic
exposed sandstone of the Caha Mountains, offering stunning
views of rolling, rock-strewn hills from the top.

Fair warning: the Beara has a lure that's hard to escape,
and it's easy to see why the region is rife with legends of
humans becoming trapped in fairy circles. Like the folks in
these stories, you may be so entranced by the Beara that
you'll find it hard to leave.

Mare's Tail Waterfall

Take a rest stop at the highest waterfall in Ireland, which cascades off the stark rock of Hungry Hill into verdant fields below.

Uragh Stone Circle

A ring of ancient megaliths set against mountains, lakes, green meadows, and a waterfall, this is one of the most magical places in Ireland.

Dursey Island

Take a break on this rugged island, accessed by a 820 ft (250 m) cable car ride over the ocean. Look down and you might spy dolphins in the waves below.

Dunboy Castle

This Celtic stronghold was destroyed in a 17th-century siege; the overgrown ruins provide a tranquil place to learn about the region's history.

Canyoning

Using a range of disciplines and skills—including rappelling, climbing, swimming and hiking—canyoners travel through a gorge, narrow valley, or river system, uncovering landscapes that would otherwise remain hidden from view. On the way, there might be the chance to jump into pools, slide down whitewater rapids, or scramble across rocky terrain. Exploring under the expert eye of a professional guide is absolutely essential, as is protective gear.

Jumping from on high into one of the many pools found in Ötztal

◁ ÖTZTAL, AUSTRIA

Prepare yourself for a challenge in an Austrian valley that offers a series of adventures for experienced canyoners.

An Alpine valley tucked away in Austria's western state of Tyrol, Ötztal feels like heaven for adventure sports enthusiasts. Alongside hundreds of mountains that are over 9,843 ft (3,000 m) in height and scores of pristine glaciers, it's also home to the powerful Ötztaler Ache, a river churning with fearsome rapids. The power of its flow has helped create deep, narrow, sheer-sided valleys, ravines, and gorges, as well as towering waterfalls and meandering water courses—a landscape perfect for canyoning.

Experts should head straight to the Auerklamm gorge, a place that is wild, ruggedly beautiful, and packed with obstacles to overcome. Here, you'll face heart-stopping jumps of up to 52 ft (16 m), dizzyingly rapid water chutes, and vertigo-inducing 131 ft (40 m) rappels down gushing cascades. There are also giant boulders as slippery as ice and tricky spray-soaked climbs with which to contend. Alongside these physical feats, there are psychological challenges to overcome, including several claustrophobically narrow swimming sections.

Periodically, the wider Ötztal valley will appear through a gap in the rocky cliffs: tiny villages surrounded by meadows, emerald-green pine forests on the lower slopes behind them, and snow-covered mountains in the background. Enjoy the views while you can—such snatched moments of calm don't last long on fast-paced canyoning expeditions through the Auerklamm gorge.

A canyoner rappelling
into Greece's iconic
Calypso gorge

△ MOUNT KISSAVOS, GREECE

Develop your canyoning skills on a Greek mountain
rich in myths and legends.

In Greek mythology, Mount Kissavos (or Mount Ossa)
was always in the shadow of neighboring Mount Olympus,
the highest peak in the country and legendary home
of the gods. But when it comes to canyoning, Kissavos
bows to no one. Cutting through its slopes, which are
thickly forested with pine, beech, and chestnut trees, is a
collection of gorges and canyons that vary widely in terms
of scenery, obstacles, and difficulty level.

   The Giannoulas canyon is a good place for first-timers
and younger canyoners to get the hang of things. Here,
you'll find a group of small—but still impressive—waterfalls
to navigate, as well as plenty of opportunities to catch
your breath and soak up the scenery. Once you've got the
canyoning basics under your belt, visit nearby Kakoskala.
With its 131 ft (40 m) cascade to rappel down and a series
of rocky terraces to scale, this canyon requires a little
more technical expertise but is still accessible for novices.

   To further test your skills, head to Calypso (or Kalypso);
this gorge was named after Greek mythology's most
famous nymph, who used her songs to captivate the hero
in Homer's epic poem the *Odyssey*. Offering superb views
of the Aegean Sea, it has an array of natural slides, numerous big jumps, and no fewer than nine waterfalls to rappel
down—the tallest is more than 230 ft (70 m) high and feeds
into a gorgeous navy-blue lagoon. Be careful, though:
much like Odysseus before you, you might end up becoming so enchanted that you won't be able to leave.

▷ NEVIDIO, MONTENEGRO

Challenge yourself on a journey through a seemingly
inaccessible canyon in the heart of Montenegro.

Carved into the gray rock of the Durmitor massif by the
unceasing flow of the pale-blue Komarnica River, this
1.9-mile (3 km) canyon is a rather forbidding prospect. In
places, the rocky gorge shrinks to less than 1.6 ft (0.5 m)
wide, while its walls soar to heights of 1,312 ft (400 m) or
more, blocking out the sun, leaching the warmth from
the water, and casting long shadows across many of the
obstacles that lie in wait. As you descend on a guided
expedition through this canyoning hot spot, there are
teeth-grittingly tight fractures to squeeze through,
bracingly cold pools to plunge into, slippery boulders
to clamber over, and icy waterfalls to rappel down. It's
fair to say that exploring this claustrophobic canyon is
not for the fainthearted—but for those brave enough
to take the plunge, a day of pure adventure awaits.

Diving from a rocky ledge
into one of the icy pools
that dot the length of the
Nevidio canyon

Conquering Nevidio

Nevidio (meaning "unseen" in the Montenegrin language) is often described as the "last conquered canyon in Europe." Until the middle of the 20th century, it was thought to be impregnable due to the incredible narrowness of its geography. In the 1950s and early 1960s, there was a series of attempts to navigate along the full length of the canyon, all of which were ultimately unsuccessful. The breakthrough finally came in August 1965 when a team of lightly equipped climbers from the city of Niksic managed to complete the task.

Mooring on calm,
glasslike waters in the
Stockholm Archipelago

Sailing

Nothing beats the serenity of sailing silently across the ocean beneath a cornflower-blue sky, hoisting your sails in the breeze, and meandering along a rocky coastline or around a remote island. Get underway by chartering a skippered yacht—or if you have sailing expertise, a "bareboat" (no crew) yacht—and heading out to sea to soak up Europe's extraordinarily diverse coastline.

▷ STOCKHOLM ARCHIPELAGO, SWEDEN

This tranquil archipelago offers curious sailors the chance to explore thousands of islands.

Scattered to the east of Sweden's capital, the Stockholm Archipelago is made up of nearly 30,000 islands, islets, and skerries. The archipelago extends 50 miles (80 km) into the blue-gray waters of the Baltic Sea, slowly transforming from larger, forested islands edged with rustic summer houses closer to the center, to small, low-lying granite rocks that evoke feelings of a Jurassic wilderness on the outer edge. When such an abundance of islands is paired with mostly flat, calm waters, it's easy to see why many Swedish sailors never go beyond the archipelago. One day, you might be sailing your small yacht through a narrow channel between pine-clad islands; on another, you could be drifting over glasslike waters lined by sandy beaches or skimming over open water as your craft loops around rugged islets. ▶

Insider Tip

Although sailing conditions in the archipelago are suitable for all levels of sailor, you'll need maps, GPS and mapping software, or an experienced skipper. This will ensure that you don't get lost or damage your boat in shallow water around the many land masses.

Ängsö

One of Sweden's first national parks, this island has more than 400 different plant species and a rich variety of birdlife, including ospreys and sea eagles.

Finnhamn

This popular island, containing several nature reserves, is home to ancient forests and lush meadows where deer, fox, and badgers roam.

Gålö

A protected reserve, this nature-rich spot is crisscrossed with hiking trails, which wind past beaches, across meadows, and through oak and pine forests.

Grinda

This pristine island, part of a nature reserve, is blessed with secluded beaches and clean, clear waters. Locals come here to sunbathe and swim.

Top One of the archipelago's traditional wooden houses
Above Heading for a dip in the calm waters off one of the islands
Left Navigating narrow passages around the rocky isles of the Stockholm Archipelago

The Original Navy Seals

During World War II, a secret—and unusual—training facility was set up on Gålö in the Stockholm Archipelago. Here, Valdemar Fellenius, a Swedish psychologist, and his small team trained seals for use in Sweden's navy. These intelligent marine mammals were taught to detect foreign submarines, mines, and torpedoes. The US and Russia later ran similar projects during the Cold War.

There are plenty of spots to drop anchor, too, from quiet moorings off uninhabited islets to bustling harbors lined with crimson-hued wooden houses. Some islands will attempt to lure you away from the water with their incredible history, including Vaxholm, home to an imposing 19th-century fortress, and Gålö, whose unique "seal station" museum recounts the role these marine mammals played in World War II. Elsewhere, you'll find pretty settlements filled with restaurants and bars and sandy stretches perfect for sunbathing; Sandön, known to locals as Sandhamn, offers both, thanks to its picturesque harbor village and beautiful beaches, such as Trouville. There are also 40 nature reserves found within the island group, where you can go flora spotting or hike through lush forests. Whether on land or water, make sure you keep your eyes peeled for the sea eagles and gray seals that call these islands home.

Sailing past Mykonos, one of the spectacular Cyclades islands

△ CYCLADES, GREECE

Scattered across the Aegean Sea, the picturesque Cyclades offer a challenge for experienced sailors.

Found southeast of the Greek mainland, the Cyclades are a collection of more than 200 arid islands based around Delos, the sacred birthplace of Apollo and Artemis. Baked golden by the sun, these rugged isles are famed for their sugar-sand beaches, architecture steeped in history, and cubic whitewashed houses that tumble down rocky hillsides. As one of the only Greek island groups that is not protected from the wind by land, the Cyclades' aquamarine waters provide a lot of fun for more experienced seafarers. This is especially true from July to September, when the seasonal Meltemi—a powerful northerly wind— whips across the Aegean, creating big waves that can then be funneled between the islands. The conditions are undoubtedly tricky—but those with strong sea legs will relish the challenge of sailing over choppy waters, cooling sea spray flying all around, as they head off to explore the next sun-baked isle.

> **"*The Cyclades' aquamarine waters provide a lot of fun for more experienced seafarers.*"**

▷ SPLIT, CROATIA

Sail from Split—Croatia's second city—for a laid-back introduction to island-hopping by yacht.

In the scattered Adriatic islands off the coast of Split, adventures on the high seas are tempered by never being far from a safe harbor, sheltered cove, or superb seafood restaurant. In the long hot summer months, calm turquoise bays protected by rugged arid hills are perfect anchorages, and once you've got the hang of "Med mooring" (reversing in, stern to the quay), you can glide between island marinas at your leisure.

From Split, sail clear of Brač—which can get busy with day-trippers—and make for sleepy Šolta, hiding in plain sight just nine nautical miles from the city. The island's south coast is lined with picture-perfect white-pebble bays lapped by cobalt waters, great for swimming and sunbathing; its north coast, meanwhile, is dotted with the seaside villages of Rogač and Stomorska, whose pretty waterside restaurants tempt you with freshly caught grilled fish and ocean views. A short hop away over shimmering seas is the crown jewel of the Dalmatian islands: hedonistic Hvar. While the island's eponymous main town can get a little crowded, its rocky north coast is wonderfully peaceful. Here, you can drop anchor and spend a lazy afternoon napping on the warmth of the sun-kissed deck, before sailing toward the pristine Pakleni Islands, found just off Hvar's southwest shore. From here, the rest of the Dalmatian coast is your oyster: why not head west to sip wines in the vineyards of wooded Vis? Or go south to reach the off-the-beaten-track islands of Lastovo, Korčula, and Mljet? Wherever you choose, one thing is certain—more easy-going sailing and impossibly beautiful Mediterranean scenery are just around the corner.

Cruising over clear cobalt waters among Croatia's Dalmatian islands

Stand-Up Paddleboarding

With its focus on the meditative pull of the paddle through the water, stand-up paddleboarding (SUP) is an ideal way to slow down and be at one with your thoughts. That's not to say it doesn't require the ability to balance and an understanding of changing weather conditions. It does. But it's as calming as it is challenging. Best of all, it doesn't take long to pick up the basics—with a good guide, you'll be ready to strike out for the horizon in no time.

▷ IJSSELMEER, NETHERLANDS

Paddle across Western Europe's largest freshwater lake, a man-made marvel of Dutch engineering.

The largest lake in the Netherlands, IJsselmeer has become a mecca for stand-up paddleboarding. Because it's closed off by the Afsluitdijk, a large dam that protects it from the Zuiderzee (part of the North Sea), conditions here are perfect for taking out a board and slowing down the pace after spending time in nearby Amsterdam. Not only can you drift along in the company of the lake's renowned birdlife, including tufted ducks and great crested grebes, but the flat landscape means you can see for miles when standing atop your board, with an uninterrupted view of the traditional towns and villages that line the water's edge. It's a scenic setting that becomes even more sublime as the sun drops over the water toward the North Sea.

Paddleboarding past Hindeloopen, a traditional town on the banks of the IJsselmeer

△ WYE VALLEY, ENGLAND/WALES

A paddleboard provides the perfect perch from which to enjoy some of Britain's prettiest riverbanks.

A paddleboarder making
their way down the Wye

To paddleboard down the Wye is to cut through a picturesque rural heartland that straddles the border of England and Wales, on a river with unspoiled banks and bends that swoop majestically. There are several launch spots for experienced paddleboarders, but beginners or those not familiar with the area should book a guided tour to help get their bearings. The river is relatively fast flowing, which makes for easy downstream paddling—and happily doesn't make it any harder to balance. This relaxed setup allows you to focus on the wonderful wildlife all around; you'll see ducks, swans, damsel and dragonflies, and if you're lucky, a kingfisher or otter. Beyond the reeds, old-growth forest and the odd sprawling country estate all add to the deep nature feel.

Leave No Trace

The wild landscape of the Wye can be easily damaged while paddleboarding, so minimize your impact by following a few simple rules. Approach riverbanks slowly, lift instead of drag your equipment over any rocks, and refrain from digging into the water weeds and gravel beds with your paddle. If you disturb any wildlife, then stop paddling until things calm down.

Going for an early morning paddleboard on the emerald waters of the Eibsee

⋀

Explore More

Lying just to the east of the Eibsee is the stunning Hollental Gorge (Hell's Valley Gorge), lined with huge cliffs and high waterfalls. You wouldn't want to take a paddleboard through here, but it's an awesome route to hike. The path is about 3 miles (5 km) long and includes narrow tunnels, overhanging walls, and stretches doused in dramatic water spray.

◁ EIBSEE, GERMANY

Envelop yourself in the grandeur of Germany's highest peak as you paddle around the sparkling waters of the Eibsee.

The Eibsee is frequently called one of the most beautiful lakes in Germany, and looking at its crystal-clear, green-hued water, densely forested banks, and rocky mountain backdrop, it's hard to disagree with that sentiment. The lake sits in the shadow of the Bavarian Alps, at the foot of Zugspitze, Germany's tallest peak—a jagged, photogenic mountain that stands 9,718 ft (2,962 m) tall. It's a spectacular spot for the scenery alone but is also a wonderful location to go stand-up paddleboarding. Not only is the Eibsee generally calm, making it a good place for first-timers to build up their confidence, but it's also over 2 miles (3 km) long, enabling more experienced paddle-boarders to test their skills and endurance by exploring the lake's outer reaches.

The pristine setting is almost too perfect to intrude upon, so paddleboarding feels like a fitting way to get around—allowing you to appreciate the Eibsee's natural treasures as unobtrusively as possible. The waters here provide a habitat for several species of fish—including pike, tench, brown and rainbow trout—as well as an array of ducks and other birdlife, which can often be glimpsed while paddling. The lake can be busy on weekends in summer, with rental kayaks, paddleboats, and swimmers to navigate around, but it's big enough that it's easy to get away from the crowds, especially if you make for the center. You can also seek sanctuary with a rest stop at one of the rocky coves or eight tree-covered islands dotted around the lake; the islands especially have a wild, backcountry feel, and it's easy to imagine yourself adrift in the middle of nowhere, far away from civilization.

After your paddle, head for Eibsee beach, which has a laid-back, Caribbean-inspired atmosphere and is a good place for a swim. Relaxing here is an idyllic way to round off the day, drinking sundowners and snacking on pretzels and *kaiserschmarrn* (locally sweetened pancakes) as you soak up evening views of the lake.

Downhill Snow Sports

Europe is the ultimate adventure park for skiers and snowboarders—a fifth of the continent is mountainous, with 10 major ranges lying between the Pyrenees and the Caucasus. Hitting the slopes at a resort brings the benefits of handy lifts and lively après-ski, but there's also scope for off-piste action away from the crowds. It's simply a case of picking your peak.

◁ LYNGEN ALPS, NORWAY

Eschew the trappings of traditional resorts in favor of a low-impact touring adventure in a magical, remote landscape.

Situated 500 miles (800 km) inside the Arctic Circle, with 60 summits over 3,280 ft (1,000 m), the Lyngen Alps form an ethereal landscape of deep-blue fjords snaking between lines of jagged snowy peaks. Enjoying good late-season snow and long, light days, the range has an almost mythical status among the ski and snowboard touring community— it's a regular haunt for ski guides from around the world, who come here once their own seasons have ended. In May and June, there's even the unique chance to ski under the midnight sun.

Touring is a world apart from traditional downhill skiing at a standard resort. For one thing, there are no lifts—you have to hike up to ski down. This gives Lyngen a wild and remote feel and means that you'll most likely have the slopes here all to yourself—the only sounds will be the pant of your breath and the squeak of fresh snow. It's undoubtedly hard work, but the fact that you have to "earn" your turns only adds to the buzz of the experience, particularly when you reach a summit. The peaks here are not especially high—the tallest is 6,014 ft (1,833 m)—so the climbs are not as physically demanding as they would be somewhere like the Alps, although you do need a good basic level of fitness. The relatively low mountain height also brings one extra benefit to the scenic fjord setting: in one day, it's easily possible to bag a summit and then ski or snowboard right down to the sea.

Skiing in solitude on the remote slopes of the Lyngen Alps in Arctic Norway

▷ VIA LATTEA, ITALY

Skiing Italy's "Milky Way" is just as spectacular
as it sounds, with sublime Alpine views and long,
picturesque trails.

From the top of the lifts, a panorama of snow-laden
valleys unfolds. You're at the roof of the Cottian Alps,
in Italy's northerly Piedmont region—but to skiers and
boarders, this snowy realm is better known as Via Lattea,
or the Milky Way.

This winter sports colossus lies at the Italy–France
border, with 273 miles (440 km) of ski trails threading
between six villages (all but one on the Italian side). The
2006 Winter Olympic Games in Turin built up excellent
infrastructure here, although uber-modern resorts in
neighboring France and Austria have since eclipsed
Via Lattea as the trendy destination of choice. No matter:
you're here for the snow and the hearty cuisine (and
perhaps the comparatively cheap lift tickets).

It's apt that Italy's Milky Way is named after a massive,
swirling galaxy. The layout of the interlinking resorts
is spiral-shaped, and the sparkling effect of sunshine
meeting snow brings to mind the stars. But for skiers and
snowboarders, the true magic is the voluminous snow:
Via Lattea receives an average of 20 ft (6 m) of fluffy
snow each winter. High above the tree line, you can soar
through fresh powder, your skis kicking up great clouds
of the white stuff. More often than not, the sky is totally
cloudless—the resort basks in almost 100 days of sunshine
every ski season.

Yes, there are blue runs for beginners, as well as
off-piste adventures for brave adrenaline seekers. But Via
Lattea truly excels for intermediate skiers, with more than
half of its runs classed red—many of them long, tree-lined
trails. One of the lengthiest extends for nearly 5 miles
(8 km)—turn by turn, you'll find a hypnotic rhythm as
you ski uninterrupted from the top of Monte Fraiteve
to San Sicario–Pariol.

Each day brings the chance to explore a different
valley. The slopes above Sauze d'Oulx are crisscrossed by
exhilarating red runs, which trickle down into cruisy blue
runs as they approach the village. It's easy to spend a

Insider Tip

It's challenging to travel green
at winter sports resorts, with
their energy-intensive ski lifts
and snow-making machines.
But in Piedmont, you can
lighten your carbon footprint
with your fork—this is the
birthplace of the Slow Food
movement, which promotes
seasonal ingredients and
sustainable food production.
Look for restaurants dis-
playing a snail logo to sample
locally sourced specialties.

whole afternoon here, slaloming past snow-laden
evergreens on the well-maintained pistes. At the top
of the range lies Sestriere, the loftiest village of all at
6,677 ft (2,035 m). Gazing out from here, you can see
mountains form a jagged horizon with an often cloudless
sky. The only way is down, carving a path across the
flanks of Monte Motta and luxuriating in the velvety
feel of snow beneath your skis.

As sunset approaches, raise an Aperol Spritz and slice
of pizza at one of the resorts' various après-ski spots—
assuming you're done with the snow, that is. As darkness
descends, floodlights flick on, illuminating the pistes for
night skiing. For skiers and revelers alike, Via Lattea
doesn't do early nights.

A snowboarder performing a
jump while descending a
run at Italy's Via Lattea

Skiing Innovation

Some of the earliest ski schools were established in Austria, and several groundbreaking ski techniques have been created in the Alps here. These include the Arlberg style, which helps skiers transition from beginners' "snowplow" turns, where your ski tips point inward, to intermediate level, where your skis remain parallel, and the wedel technique, characterized by short, swift parallel turns.

Right Alpine wooden buildings in Saalbach-Hinterglemm
Below Cruising down the sunny slopes of the Austrian Alps

▷ SAALBACH-HINTERGLEMM, AUSTRIA

With epic mountains and efficient infrastructure, skiing in Saalbach-Hinterglemm is a delight.

Southwest of Salzburg, the ski zone of Saalbach-Hinterglemm has 168 miles (270 km) of pistes unfurling across the Austrian Alps. The snowy peaks here can be skied in either direction, meaning you can plot a different mountain-hopping route each day. Wherever you ski, spectacular views follow. From the top of the Zwölferkogel alone (a mountain reached by gondola), the selection of red, blue, or black runs will lead you in a glorious zigzag toward your choice of Schattberg's expansive plains, the tree-lined Lengau valley or perhaps down to Hinterglemm for a fortifying *gluhwein* (mulled wine).

It's not just the sublime views that make skiing here so enjoyable—the infrastructure plays a part, too. High-speed, high-capacity lifts ensure there are no sluggish queues, maximizing your time on the snow. This is good news for skiers of all levels, but especially beginners, who will be schussing far and wide in no time. The glow of *gemütlichkeit* (good cheer) has never come more easily.

△ KOPAONIK, SERBIA

Strap on your skis and take to the pistes
in a nature-rich national park.

Kopaonik is Serbia's most famous ski resort—and for
good reason. Located on the mountain range of the same
name, at the foot of its highest peak, this is a beautiful
area of well-cared-for slopes and swooping tree-lined
runs. The surrounding plateau was declared a national
park in 1981, its coniferous forests harboring golden
eagles and European wildcats. There are 34 miles (55 km)
of family-friendly runs, the majority of them located south
of town, staggered up the slopes of Pančićev vrh. Start
your day by taking a chairlift to the top, peeking into
neighboring Kosovo, then slowly work your way back
down to town, cruising among snowcapped spruces that
are home to partridges, shrikes, and all other manner of
birdlife that calls these protected pistes home.

Above Skiers and a snowboarder on a slope at
Kopaonik, lined by towering pine trees

Wild Camping

Wild camping—pretty much any experience where you pitch your tent outside of a traditional campsite—is pure freedom. Yes, it entails sacrificing a bit of luxury (wave goodbye to taps and toilets), but in exchange you get to escape the frenetic modern world with a night amid spectacular scenery. All that's needed is some trusty camping gear, a desire to "leave no trace," and a good grasp of the wild camping rules for your chosen spot.

Top Walking in the Cairngorms
Bottom left Sunset illuminating a grassy meadow
Bottom right Walking boots and a kettle sitting lakeside

◁ CAIRNGORMS, SCOTLAND

Scotland's biggest national park lures wild campers with its untamed beauty, diverse wildlife, and sense of remote tranquility.

Few would deny it: Scotland is the best place in Europe to go wild camping. This isn't just because of its stunning landscapes, as impressive as the Caribbean-style beaches, inky-blue lakes, and wind-scoured mountains undoubtedly are. It's also thanks to the country's progressive Land Reform Act (2003), a law that allows adventurous souls to pitch up on most unenclosed land provided that they "leave no trace." True, there are a handful of restricted areas—a small number of locations, for example, require camping permits—but for the most part, Scotland is wonderfully free to roam. You can camp here year-round, too, although winter is definitely best left to hardy, experienced campers with the right gear. ▶

Leave No Trace

Make sure you wild camp responsibly by checking out the Scottish Outdoor Access Code before you go *(www.outdooraccess-scotland.scot)*. This sets out the rights and responsibilities of wild campers and includes such things as removing any trace of your tent pitch and taking away your litter.

Camping on the edge of a tree-lined lake in Cairngorms National Park

Spotter's Guide

Red Deer

Scotland's largest deer are distinguished by their chestnut coats with pale tail and rump; the stags also have large, branching antlers.

Red Squirrels

Although extremely rare, red squirrels can be spotted in the Cairngorms. Keep an eye out for their copper-colored fur and tufted ears and tail.

Pine Martens

Members of the weasel family, these nocturnal creatures have rounded ears, long bodies, and dark brown coats with a creamy patch at the throat.

Ospreys

These majestic birds have a white head with a brown eye stripe. Females are up to 20 percent larger than males, with a brown patch on their chest.

Above Heather blanketing a field
Right Waking up to views across a tranquil lake

To truly lose yourself in Scotland's wilderness, head to the Cairngorms in the Highlands. Covering 1,748 sq miles (4,527 sq km), this expansive national park is twice the size of England's Lake District but receives far fewer visitors—meaning that you're more likely to find a quiet place to pitch up. And when it comes to actually picking a spot, you're thoroughly spoiled for choice. Where else can you choose between a glacier-scoured mountain plateau, the glowing purple heather of rugged moorland, a sheltered glen watched over by pockets of deep-green Caledonian pine, or grassy banks near a tranquil lake or winding river?

As you make camp, keep an eye out for wildlife—the park is home to thousands of different species. Spy red deer roaming through rugged valleys, the heads of the stags topped with majestic antlers; glimpse golden eagles and ospreys wheeling overhead; and spot red squirrels and pine martens darting between the trees. The only resident you'll

not want to see are the clouds of unwanted—yet ever-attentive—midges. Try to make camp in a breezy spot, bring repellent, and cover up your arms and legs; these tiny flying insects have a vicious bite.

As evening descends, spark up your stove (avoid open fires as they pose a wildfire risk) and listen to the noises of the landscape. Away from civilization, nature's soundtrack—the soft rustling of pine needles, the gurgling chatter of a burn, the occasional hooting of an owl—seems to be gently amplified. A lack of light pollution here means that—clouds allowing—you might be able to spy a glittering mass of stars blazing above. Take some time to gaze upward before diving for the welcome warmth of your sleeping bag as the temperature drops.

In the morning, after a fortifying traditional Scottish breakfast (porridge, of course), it's time to pack up your tent and head deeper into the mountains. Who knows where you'll find tomorrow night's campsite?

LOFOTEN ISLANDS, NORWAY

Want to escape civilization? Set up a beachside camp on this isolated archipelago.

You can't get much more remote than the Lofoten Islands—rising shardlike from the icy Norwegian Sea, this collection of rocky isles is located 186 miles (300 km) into the Arctic Circle. While much of the land here is either too boggy or rocky to make a perfect pitch, a handful of beaches along the northern coast beckon intrepid campers. One of the best is Bunes; overlooked by iron-colored peaks, this sweep of golden sand is backed by springy grassy dunes and lapped by Mediterranean-like waters (in color, if not temperature). As night falls, simply sit back and look skyward for the dancing northern lights.

Top left Camping on the stunning coast of Norway's remote Lofoten Islands

LAHEMAA NATIONAL PARK, ESTONIA

Camp with a sprinkling of luxury in Estonia's largest and oldest national park.

Home to ancient old-growth forests, sandy seashores, and pond-punctuated peat bogs, Lahemaa feels a million miles away from the modern world. It would be easy to assume that wild camping here was going to be of the rough-and-ready variety—but you'd be wrong. Dotted throughout the park are a number of free campsites that come complete with all the frills— outdoor fireplaces, picnic tables, and sometimes even (joy of joys) toilets. Forested Juminda campsite, perched on the park's westernmost peninsula, is a great place to light up a crackling fire, stick on an *Ühepajatoit* (Estonian stew), and celebrate the day's end with spiced *glögi*.

Bottom left One of the walking tracks leading through the forests of Estonia's Lahemaa National Park

ARCHIPELAGO NATIONAL PARK, FINLAND

Get back to nature with a night spent on a remote Finnish island.

Life in Finland is firmly lived outdoors—and it's easy to see why. Not only is the country a place of stunning natural beauty, it also enshrines in law the ability to roam freely in nature (known as *Jokamiehenoikeudet* or "Everyman's Right"). Make like a local and take advantage of this freedom at Archipelago National Park. Reached by kayak, this watery labyrinth is made up of over 2,000 mostly uninhabited islands, many of which are topped with lush green foliage. Hunker down by the stony shore and spend the evening foraging for berries and finding wood for a campfire, before being lulled to sleep by the sound of the sea.

Top right Sunset over Archipelago National Park in southwest Finland

DARTMOOR NATIONAL PARK, ENGLAND

Disappear into the untamed heart of Devon for a night of quiet isolation.

There's a bleak and wild beauty to Dartmoor. Vast swathes of open moorland—topped by dramatic granite tors—seem to stretch endlessly into the distance, cut through by wooded river valleys and dotted with boggy mires. Even by day, this national park can feel deserted, with only the occasional walker or herd of sturdy Dartmoor ponies to be seen. At night, you're almost certain to have the setting all to yourself— somewhat surprising, as it's the only place in England where you can legally wild camp (for up to two nights). Pitch up atop one of the rocky hills and watch as the setting sun illuminates the earthy colors of this brooding landscape.

Bottom right A tent pitched in the heart of England's rugged Dartmoor National Park

Hot Springs

There's something exciting, elemental even, about bathing in a hot spring—shedding your clothes (often when the air temperature would tell you to do otherwise) and lowering yourself into a natural bath that's been heated deep inside the bowels of the Earth. Since at least the Neolithic era, humankind has recognized the benefits of a good soak—the purifying powers that geothermal waters possess and the drowsy contentment that comes from cocooning yourself within their warmth. Step into the steam and reconnect with nature at its most essential.

The cyan-blue waters of Saturnia, bubbling over pearly travertine rocks

◁ SATURNIA, ITALY

Take a dip in the midst of the Tuscan hills, where the thermal waters have been flowing for well over 3,000 years.

If Tuscany wasn't Italy's most romantic region already, then the beautiful hot springs at Saturnia would surely seal the deal. Heated deep beneath nearby Monte Amiata, the thermal waters rise just to the south of town, flowing along a creek that ambles through fields dotted with gnarly old olive trees before tumbling over a series of rocky travertine terraces. It's here, in the milky blue pools of the freely accessible Cascate del Mulino, that you should do as the Romans did: lie back and let the healing waters work their magic.

The Romans—and the Etruscans and Greeks before them—recognized the curative properties of Saturnia's springs. These waters are rich in minerals, especially sulfur (don't be put off by the slightly eggy whiff), and are known to revitalize your skin, improve circulation, and relieve muscle pain and arthritis. They can work wonders for the mind as well—the surging waterfall and mesmerizing flow of water over the sculpted ledges provide a hypnotic background to tune in to as you tune out.

It's easy to stay in the pools all day, but make sure you also venture farther along the river for an exfoliating mud bath, smearing yourself in sulfurous sludge—coat evenly and bake in the hot Tuscan sun (being careful not to burn). Keep the relaxation going even after you leave the water, by picnicking on a lunch of local delicacies (cured ham, herby Pecorino, fresh olives) on the banks of the river.

Explore More

Lying just 31 miles (50 km) southeast of Reykjavík, Reykjadalur makes a more easily accessible alternative to Landmannalaugar. You'll have to hike to get to the hot spring, but the walk is easy and the landscape is extraordinary— an emerald river valley with belching mud pots and billows of steam wafting into the sky.

▷ LANDMANNALAUGAR, ICELAND

Iceland's awe-inspiring wilderness makes a primeval setting for these middle-of-nowhere hot springs, accessible only on foot or with a 4WD.

Iceland isn't known as the Land of Fire and Ice for nothing. Formed by volcanic eruptions and shaped by the ongoing battle between the North American and Eurasian plates, it's an alien landscape of icecaps and lava tubes, black-sand beaches, and spewing geysers. And there's no more relaxing way to take in all this epic scenery than from the soothing waters of a bubbling hot spring, warmed to a toasty temperature by the magma beneath you.

The most spectacular surroundings for a dip are at Landmannalaugar, the "People's Pools," which lie 112 miles (180 km) east of Reykjavík in Iceland's unforgiving interior. A rugged landscape of black lava fields, this whole region is a haven for walking, and the pools are often visited by groups of seasoned hikers, either enjoying a well-earned soak after tackling the paths up nearby Brennisteinsalda or Bláhnjúkur, or steeling themselves for the strenuous Laugavegur Trail (which runs from here to Þórsmörk, 34 miles [54 km] away to the southwest).

Set against a kaleidoscopic backdrop of rolling rhyolite mountains—painted a spectrum of brightly colored quartz and daubed in the yellows and reds of sulfur and iron—the pools are surrounded by vivid green grass that stands out against the barren gravel plain. Start with an invigorating plunge into the cold spring, at the end of the wooden boardwalk, and then work your way into the warmth, wading through the water until you find the perfect spot in which to slowly submerge yourself.

Top right Looking over Iceland's colorful rhyolite mountains
Above Bathing in the steamy Landmannalaugar hot spring

▽ BËNJA THERMAL BATHS, ALBANIA

Heal your mind and body in the infinity-pool hot springs of southeast Albania.

Deep within Albania's Fir of Hotova National Park, the River Langarica flows a cyan blue. Snaking a line through the eroded limestone cliffs of Langarica Canyon, it carries its thermal waters northward from the town of Përmet. At various stages along the way, the water has been diverted into round stone pools, some within the canyon itself, others—known as the Bënja Thermal Baths—at the foot of a romantic arched bridge that the Ottomans built. People come here to cure their ailments; each pool is supposedly beneficial for a particular complaint, from acne to rheumatism. But if nothing else, the views will soothe your soul—across a rocky landscape, streaked with Macedonian firs and fragrant juniper trees, to the snowcapped ridges beyond.

> **"** *If nothing else, the views will soothe your soul.* **"**

Above Relaxing in the Bënja Thermal Baths, under the arch of the old Ottoman bridge

Bouldering

Bouldering is rock climbing's feisty little brother. Considered to be
"low level"—usually 16 ft (5 m) or below—the sport, in its purest
form, is simply scaling a ball of rock. The only pieces of gear required
are climbing shoes for grip and mats to prevent serious injury if you
fall. You'll also need to bring a bit of brain power—bouldering climbs
are known as "problems," with their short heights posing technical
challenges that require considered thought as well as strength.

◁ FONTAINEBLEAU, FRANCE

The holy grail of bouldering, Fontainebleau has
a baffling variety of boulders strewn throughout
an enchanting forest.

If this beautiful world was sculpted by higher powers,
Fontainebleau—or Font, as it's affectionately known—is
surely proof that the creators were climbers. In fact, the
unique sandstone boulders found here are so perfect for
the sport, they'll make you second-guess whether they're
completely natural or not.

Varying in height from 6ft (1.8 m) to as much as 20ft
(6 m), these world-famous rock formations come in every
shape imaginable—monolithic slabs worn smooth by the
elements, gnarled arches pocked with cavities, and huge
orbs that look like part of a giant game of marbles. Each
one is unique and requires a distinctive blend of powerful
yet precise climbing, combining subtle footwork and
problem-solving on smooth, finger-forgiving rock. ▶

Bouldering in the shady
surrounds of the Forêt
de Fontainebleau

Leave No Trace

Although climbing is
welcomed in Fontainebleau,
sustainability is key—the
sandstone here is particularly
vulnerable to erosion. Wiping
sand from your shoes and
brushing holds before
climbing will help preserve
the rock. It's also important to
wait until rocks are dry from
rain and take heed of local
advice or signage.

A Birthplace for Bouldering

The origins of bouldering date back to the 1930s, when French climber Pierre Allain and his gang of "Bleausards"—specialists in climbing at Fontainebleau—began to draw attention to the area's small but powerful boulders. (Allain even invented the first rubber-soled climbing shoe for the technical footwork.) By the 1950s, Font's first circuits and bouldering guidebooks had been created, laying the foundations for the modern sport.

Most of the climbing spots are submerged within the Forêt de Fontainebleau, a densely packed forest brimming with wildlife and vegetation. Hundreds of closely linked areas offer more than 30,000 bouldering problems, many of which have marked and graded climbing circuits that help guide you around—something rare for outdoor bouldering. There's everything from low-lying traverses just perfect for beginners to towering highballs that lure in the pros.

Despite the utter brilliance of the climbing, your surroundings come close to stealing the show. Toasty French sun pierces through the trees, choirs of birds sing in the canopy above, and an earthy smell of pine cones fills the air. Nowhere else in the world could you find such an astounding variety of bouldering in quite so idyllic a setting.

Working on a problem across an arched boulder in Fontainebleau

▽ PRILEP, NORTH MACEDONIA

Make your mark on an up-and-coming bouldering hot spot in North Macedonia.

Given that the hills around Prilep look like they've been hit by an asteroid storm, it's little wonder that the city is a rising star in the bouldering world. Arriving on the scene in the early 2000s, Prilep was initially the preserve of in-the-know locals, before drawing international attention after Slovenian climber Rok Šisernik paid a visit to the area in 2009.

Even though it's building a strong reputation, you'll often find Prilep's boulder fields quiet, with space to work new problems on the granite rocks. Granite usually goes hand-in-hand with a tough, "crimpy" climbing style, and the small, sharp handholds here are no exception. They'll test your finger strength and footwork to the max.

Above Granite formations on the verdant hills surrounding the North Macedonian city of Prilep

▷ ALBARRACÍN, SPAIN

Offering a huge variety of problems for all abilities, this idyllic spot is a great place to find your feet when bouldering outdoors for the first time.

Perched precariously on a hilltop above the Guadalaviar river in eastern Spain, the spectacular medieval village of Albarracín—declared a National Monument in 1961—is well worth a visit in and of itself. Its narrow, cobbled streets are lined with red-brick houses that haven't changed for centuries, and the 9th-century castle looks as if it grew straight out of the cliff edge. Undoubtedly scenic, this craggy setting also makes the village a haven for climbers, with a huge bouldering playground lying right on the doorstep, in the surrounding mountains and national park.

The boulders are located in a large area of lush pine forest, just a few minutes' drive north of the village. The shapes of the holds on the sandstone rocks are often relatively similar to those you'll find at indoor gyms, and many of the routes offer dynamic moves that aren't too technical. If the prospect of taking the plunge from indoor to outdoor bouldering seems daunting, Albarracín is the ideal place to give it a go.

The conditions here are unbeatable. Dry mountain air and little rainfall usually means plenty of grip on the rock. And, with around 2,000 routes, Albarracín is far more than just an outdoor-climbing transition zone. Its world-class problems attract plenty of serious climbers. Of course, this inevitably means that Albarracín is popular. But all you need is to walk 20 minutes into the forest, and you'll be rewarded with empty areas and yet more fantastic climbs.

Insider Tip

The forest at Albarracín is part of the larger protected area of Pinares de Rodeno (Rodeno Pine Forests), which is home to a large variety of bird species. While out bouldering, keep your eyes peeled for wrens, crossbills, hawks, booted eagles, and chickadees. Climbing is banned in nesting areas, so check the signs for the latest updates.

Right and far right Climbing on boulders in the pine forest just north of Albarracín
Below The medieval village of Albarracín in the early evening

Wild Swimming

Taking a dip outdoors is utterly invigorating. The cool embrace of a lake, river, or the sea makes your skin tingle and clears your mind, bringing with it a deep sense of calm that lasts long after you've left the water. Happily, you don't need much to go wild swimming—a towel and a swimming costume or wet suit will usually do—although it's important to know how to access your chosen swim spot and stay safe in the water.

◁ GIOLA LAGOON, THASSOS, GREECE

Dive into the sparkling azure waters of this teardrop-shaped cliffside pool.

Greece has a strong line in spectacular wild-swimming spots, but few can match the majesty of Giola Lagoon. Tucked into the cliffs on the southern shores of Thassos, with long views out over the sparkling Aegean, this remote pool's allure is immediately obvious—warm, salty water that glows turquoise in the summer sun; high cliffs that are perfect for daredevils looking to make a spectacular entrance; and handy rocks that are perfect for laying out a towel to sunbathe and dry off afterward. With easy access from the rocks at one end, it's not just for divers and jumpers (who you'll need to keep an eye out for); the wide sweep of the pool makes it the perfect place for languid breaststroke and time spent floating on your back with the sunlight dancing on the surface.

Swimming in the spectacular Giola Lagoon on Greece's Thassos Island

Landmarks

Llyn Idwal

This easy-to-access lake is set in a bowl of rock peppered with boulder fields; Sir Edmund Hillary trained on the slabs here before conquering Everest.

Llyn Eiddew-Bach

This large tarn is located near the stunning stone circle of Bryn Cader Faner, in the remote Northern Rhinog Mountains east of Harlech.

Llyn Du'r Arddu

Tylwyth Teg (Welsh fairies) are said to inhabit Du'r Arddu, a tempting tarn that can be reached from the Llanberis Path up Snowdon.

Llyn Cau

A 1,150 ft (350 m) ascent up the Minffordd Path (which eventually ends at the summit of Cadair Idris) leads to this dramatic, cliffside glacial lake.

Left The stunning Llyn Idwal
Below Taking a relaxing dip
Bottom Enjoying a tranquil
sunset swim

◁ SNOWDONIA, WALES

Take a dip in a high-altitude glacial tarn nestled
within the wilds of Snowdonia.

Tarns—*llyn* in Welsh—are small mountain lakes that were
formed when glaciers retreated after the last Ice Age.
These peaceful bodies of water—with their singsong-
sounding names like Llyn Idwal, Llyn Eiddew-Bach, Llyn
Du'r Arddu, and Llyn Cau—are dotted around Snowdonia.
Reaching the still, clear waters, nestled in the scoop of
rugged, rocky amphitheaters, can be as challenging as the
swim itself—you'll often need to hike up steep unmarked
tracks through remote ice-sculpted landscapes. But the
journey is all part of the attraction. As you wade, you
feel the worries of the world slide away; Snowdonia's chilly
waters might be toe numbing (especially in winter), but they
feel cool and fresh against your skin. You kick off and glide
silently, swimming to whatever rhythm feels good to you,
and afterward, when your body is clumsy and numb, the
afterglow and sense of achievement radiates warmth
from your chest, lifting your mood as you raise your eyes
to a mountainscape hundreds of millions of years old.

Even better, since Snowdonia is a Dark Sky Reserve,
it's great for a bit of night swimming. Floating in an inky-
black pool on a clear night, looking up at stars and nebulae
(bright clouds of gas and dust) that are undimmed and
undiminished by light pollution, you'll feel both small
and powerful.

▷ LAKE BLED, SLOVENIA

Few stunning swimming spots are as easy to access
as this heavenly lake on the edge of the Julian Alps.

Tear-shaped Lake Bled is a wild swim with a difference.
As Slovenia's most popular tourist destination—Bled town
is less than 45 minutes by car from the capital Ljubljana—
this site is a far cry from the remote lakes and hard-to-
reach swimming spots usually favored by cold-water
enthusiasts. But the scenery is just as spectacular. This
is one of Europe's most picturesque lakes—watched over
by the soaring Karavanke Mountains, Bled's shimmering
emerald-green waters are encircled by verdant trees and
punctuated by the forested Bled Island.

This pretty islet—home to the iconic 17th-century
Pilgrimage Church of the Assumption of Mary—is the
obvious target for great swimmers. Set off from the pon-
toon directly below Bled Castle on the lake's northeast
shore—natural thermal springs around here warm the lake
to a pleasant 73°F (23°C) in summer—and start scything
through the water. It's around 45 minutes' swim to the
church, give or take a few minutes to detour around the
pletna boats that ferry visitors to and from the island all
day. But take your time and enjoy the beautiful backdrop:
rich green fir trees rolling away to a horizon of snow-
dusted mountain peaks. As you swim, it's easy to see
why the Slovene poet France Prešeren described Bled
as a "second Eden."

The Wishing Bell

The bell that regularly rings out from the
church in the middle of Lake Bled is said to
have been cast by Pope Clement VII, in honor
of a widow that once lived in Bled Castle.
After her husband died, Poliksena Kreigh
used up all of her gold and silver on
a memorial bell, only for a storm to sink it
en route to the church; the devastated widow
then fled to Rome to become a nun. The pope
heard of her story and sent a new bell to
Bled, decreeing that anyone ringing it
would have their wishes granted.

Jumping into the warm,
turquoise waters of
tree-lined Lake Bled

Mud Bathing

Exorbitantly priced mud baths can be found at spas around the world, but the Earth has been offering up this particular beauty treatment for free for millennia. And what you'll sacrifice in luxury by taking a dunk outside, you'll reap in organic health benefits: the healing qualities of mud bathing include everything from improving skin conditions and the function of the central nervous system to providing relief from chronic ailments. It's all about knowing the best spots at which to get a little mucky.

▷ VULCANO, ITALY

Soak in warm natural mud baths on a volcanic island in the Tyrrhenian Sea.

Although it takes its moniker from the fiery Roman god Vulcan (and in turn lends its name to the word "volcano"), the Aeolian Island of Vulcano hasn't erupted since 1890. The biggest danger you're likely to face from bathing in its natural mud pools, which sit in a nest of rocks overlooking the island's northeast coast, is smelling of sulfur for a couple of days. It's more than worth it, though—silky smooth skin is almost guaranteed, while many swear by the soothing effect of the mineral-rich mud on inflamed joints and creaky bones. Plus, the experience is supremely relaxing. The mud is lovely and warm, and the views over the sea, the rugged neighboring island of Lipari ,and the green-topped cliffs of the Tyrrhenian Coast, in the distance, are spectacular.

Above Enjoying the therapeutic properties of a thermal mud pool on the Italian island of Vulcano
Right Looking over Vulcano's steaming landscape

Above Bathers caked in mineral-
rich mud at Lake Techirghiol
Right The shore of Lake
Techirghiol in Romania

▷ LAKE TECHIRGHIOL, ROMANIA

Tap into the healing properties of Romania's largest
saltwater lake and you'll emerge with a newfound
respect for Mother Nature's restorative powers.

There is surely no finer way of tipping your hat to nature
than scooping its bounty into your palms and slathering
yourself in it from forehead to toe. That's the ritual that
draws well-being seekers in their thousands to Lake
Techirghiol—a vast, intensely saline lake on the edge of
the seaside resort of Eforie Nord. This part of the Black
Sea coast (often referred to as the Romanian Riviera)
is a jumble of sandy beaches, bath-warm seas, and the
stunning, UNESCO-listed Danube Delta. The sanatorium
here was established in 1899, and since then the lake's
dark mud has provided relief to those in need. The warm,
shiny, smearable stuff is dense with minerals and organic
matter, much of it formed over time from decomposing
flora and fauna—far more rejuvenating than it sounds and
sustainable, too, given that the sediment itself is
constantly regenerating.

Once you've paid for admission to the lake, you'll find
changing rooms in which to tug on your swimming gear
and a beach divided into two sections: one for covered
bathing and one for those wanting a nudist experience.
Rich, treacly mud is sourced from the deepest parts of
the lake and set out on the beach in pails in order for
visitors to help themselves. You simply anoint yourself
with the unctuous substance and then let it dry, before
taking a cleansing swim in the salty waters of the lake to
wash it all off.

Although often steeped in sunshine, you'll find the
lake at its most beautiful on a windy day. Its name derives
from the Turkish Tekirgöl, meaning "Striped Lake"; so
potent is the salinity of the water, that when the wind
blows, bold white salt stripes materialize on the surface.
And while this is certainly not a place of high-octane
activity—there's very little to observe but the passing
seabirds and the shimmer of the sun on the glassy
waters—it really is a beautiful spot at which to snatch
a little calm from life's frenzy.

▽ LAKE ATANASOVSKO, BULGARIA

This vast lake, with its strikingly rosy hue, is a haven for wildlife and wellness-seekers alike.

While the pink lakes of Western Australia or Mexico's Yucatán Peninsula might get all the Instagram glory, far lesser known, but no less spectacular, is Lake Atanasovsko on Bulgaria's Black Sea coast. While only part of the lake is actually pink, its hue is entirely natural: a result of the microscopic brine shrimp that live in these extremely salty waters. Take a dip and slap the healing mud across your limbs, then scurry across to the Black Sea (a mere 330 ft [100 m] away) to wash it all off. There'll be plenty to watch while you soak in the lake; Atanasovsko is also an important site for wildlife, creating a rich environment for migrating birds and the largest colony of flamingos in Bulgaria, as well as plenty of mammals, including otters and jackals.

The Legend of Tekir

Legend has it that a blind old man named Tekir once came to the shore of Lake Techirghiol with his donkey and got stuck. As Tekir struggled in the mud, it dawned on him that his eyes could see light again and that his feet, which had stopped working years ago, were beginning to move once more. When people found out, they rushed to bathe in the "healing" lake. Today, a statue of Tekir and his donkey stands in town.

Soaking in the pink waters of Lake Atanasovsko, famed for its medicinal mud

Bird-Watching

The act of bird-watching is, by definition, to attune yourself to nature—throwing off the demands of time and schedule to observe the rhythms and movements of the wild. You don't need much to pursue birding in its most basic form (though a pair of binoculars will help immensely), just patience enough to wait for the drama of the wild to cross your path and a keen eye willing to observe the small details that differentiate one species from another.

Left The jagged limestone peaks of the Picos de Europa
Below A bearded vulture standing next to a group of griffon vultures

◁ PICOS DE EUROPA, SPAIN

Admire bearded vultures soaring above the sheer rock walls of the Picos de Europa range.

If you asked a bearded vulture (aka lammergeier) to design its dream home, the result might well be the Picos de Europa. The wildflower-spangled meadows of this spectacular limestone massif, grazed each summer by sheep and goats, provide food—this magnificent raptor's favorite dish is animal bone. And the surrounding cliffs are pocked with caves, which make ideal sites for bearded vulture nests as they're surrounded by rocks on which to crack femurs. It's not particularly surprising, then, that (with the help of a groundbreaking reintroduction program) this threatened species is burgeoning here. If you're lucky, while out hiking you might spy its distinctive diamond-wedge tail among the griffon vultures that soar alongside the cliffs of vertiginous Cares Gorge, or elsewhere above the massif's valleys and meadows.

▷ MYKINES, FAROE ISLANDS, DENMARK

With their colorful striped beaks and bright orange feet, puffins never fail to delight—and on windswept Mykines, you can see them in their thousands.

Deep in the North Atlantic, a volcanic archipelago rises up from the writhing waters roughly midway between Norway and Iceland. This far-flung cluster of 18 rocky islands, otherwise known as the Faroes, is home to some of Europe's most striking landscapes—and some of its most diverse birdlife. Towering cliffs and sea stacks teem with fulmars, kittiwakes, guillemots, razorbills, and skuas—to name just a few of the 300 species found here. But it is the captivating Faroese or Atlantic puffin that really steals the show.

These colorful seabirds, with their wistful eyes and large red, yellow, and black bills, are sometimes referred to as "parrots of the sea." Puffins spend most of the year on the water, overwintering on the icy Atlantic surf by floating in large flocks known as "rafts." The only time they return to land is the summer, when they breed and raise their young (known as pufflings)—making this the ideal time to observe them in large numbers.

Mykines, the westernmost island of the Faroes, is home to a large colony of puffins and is a wonderful place to observe these beguiling birds. With its clutch of colorful dwellings, wave-battered cliffs, and frothing ocean views, the remote, car-free island is deserving of a visit for the scenery alone. If you're there for only the day, the best way to see the puffins is on the 4-mile (6 km) round hike to Holmur Lighthouse on the islet of Mykineshólmur, at the island's far western tip. The trail—which must be followed strictly to avoid disturbing wildlife—is postcard-perfect, but it's the flocks of puffins that elevate the experience from idyllic to magical.

During the hike, you'll spot anything from one or two puffins hopping and chatting along to groups of up to a dozen birds gossiping vigorously in the grass. They begin appearing in ones or twos shortly after leaving the village, but once the trail enters an area called Lambi, just before the footbridge to Mykineshólmur, the seabirds begin to appear en masse. Thousands of the comical little charmers ply these steep grassy slopes, where they dig their nesting burrows. They flutter in and out from their nests, moving dried grass around and skipping out to sea to fish. After spending even just a few moments in their company, it is easy to see why puffins are one of the best-loved birds in the world.

Spotter's Guide

Gannets
To the south of the lighthouse is a large colony of gannets. The younger birds are brown while adults are white with black wingtips.

Great Skuas
The great skua is not afraid of humans and is known for its aggressive nature. From afar, they look dark, but their white wings flash when in flight.

Leach's Storm Petrel
Mykines is the Faroes' only known breeding site for this small seabird. As they can be seen only at night, you'll have to stay on the island to spot them.

Fulmars
The most common breeding bird in the Faroe Islands, the gray-and-white northern fulmar resembles a gull and is also related to the albatross.

Above An Atlantic puffin, with its characteristic black-and-white plumage and colorful beak
Right Puffins nesting on the cliffs of Mykines, the westernmost of the Faroe Islands

◁ DANUBE DELTA, ROMANIA

This biosphere reserve is Romania's top spot for bird-watchers, with thousands of migratory birds flocking to its marshlands.

The mighty Danube River meanders for a staggering 1,770 miles (2,850 km) from its source in Germany, before finally emptying into the Black Sea at Romania's Danube Delta. A haven for wildlife along much of its route, the river saves its crowning glory for its final farewell. The marshes and lakes of the delta provide a habitat for no less than 312 bird species and have been designated a UNESCO Biosphere Reserve since 1998.

It's possible to spot a range of birdlife from the hiking and cycling paths that surround this aquatic wonderland, but the most enthralling encounters are had on the water: leisurely eco-cruises offer unimpeded views of the delta's feathered inhabitants as they preen in the temperate waters and guzzle the abundant crustaceans. As your boat glides across the water, you'll see huge dragonflies hovering above reed beds and hear the splash of marsh frogs leaping from lily pads. But it's the birdlife that elicits gasps, with long-legged ibis and graceful cormorants among the menagerie of waterfowl that can be found here year-round—along with hundreds more species that arrive during the annual migration seasons.

In spring, Dalmatian and great white pelicans descend en masse to embark on a summer feeding frenzy. You can often hear these enormous white birds before you see them: honking cacophonously, beating their wings and scooping fish into their bills with a triumphant splash. Come winter, striking red-breasted geese fly in from Siberia, entertaining rapt bird-watchers as they cavort in the shallows and snooze in the swamps. There's certainly no danger that you'll leave the delta feeling disappointed— during the peak of the migration seasons, up to 250,000 birds can be seen each day.

Top left A red-breasted goose at the Danube Delta in winter
Top right A great white pelican scooping a fish into its bill
Bottom Enjoying close-up views of pelicans on a cruise of the delta

▽ LOFOTEN ISLANDS, NORWAY

Witness the striking majesty of the sea eagle, one of Europe's largest birds.

The Lofoten Islands are a veritable playground of inky sea fjords from which glittering gray granite mountains rise to the sky. It's a fitting home for the white-tailed eagle—one of the largest birds of prey found in Europe, with a wingspan of over 7 ft (2 m).

You may catch a lucky glimpse of the eagles from terra firma, but to truly experience the birds in their resplendent glory, book a sea eagle safari to the Trollfjorden, a narrow inlet of sea. The ride—in a rigid inflatable boat that pummels the waves with spectacular abandon—is just as much a part of the experience as the eagles that come swooping down, their great wings and dark plumage stark against the snowy backdrop. What at first look like dots on the horizon quickly loom large as they dive down to catch the fish thrown by the boatsman, the birds' telltale white heads and tail feathers in stark contrast to the bright yellow of their beak and claws.

A white-tailed eagle in flight between the cliffs of Trollfjorden in the Lofoten Islands

A towering
ice formation
in Slovenia

Ice
Climbing

There are parts of Europe where it can get cold enough for long enough that the biting tendrils of winter turn waterfalls to ice, freezing them midflow into curtains of crystallized white. These fantastical scenes are the fairy-tale backdrops for ice climbing. As extreme sports go, scaling a giant sheet of ice using pickaxes and a pair of crampons has got to be right up there—only adventurous souls need read on.

◁ MLAČCA GORGE, SLOVENIA

Small but perfectly formed, the icefalls in Mlačca Gorge make an excellent introduction to ice climbing.

Wild and rugged, dotted with mountain lakes and run through by rivers of turquoise, Slovenia's Julian Alps are every bit as magnificent as their more famous namesake to the west. Their craggy peaks dominate Triglav National Park, named after the country's highest mountain and a symbol of Slovenian identity—Mount Triglav even takes pride of place on the national flag. It's against this hallowed backdrop that you'll find Mlačca Gorge, whose three waterfalls freeze over for a short but satisfying winter season each December. The solid sheet, peppered with great cauliflowers of ice, is a startling sight, but it's easy enough to ascend—you'll see children as young as 10 scrambling to the top. Don your crampons, rope up, and start ice-climbing your way after them.

▷ RJUKAN, NORWAY

Tackle hundreds of spectacular icefalls in the frosted valleys and frigid forests of southern Norway.

For nearly six months of the year, the residents of Rjukan, in Norway's Telemark region, don't see the sun. The town lies at the bottom of a narrow valley, and the surrounding mountains block out the sunlight from September to March. While this is bad news for locals, it's great news for outdoor enthusiasts, who flock here from across the world to enjoy some of the best ice climbing in Northern Europe—the lack of light, combined with consistent subzero temperatures, sees the valley filled with hundreds of frozen waterfalls, sometimes up to several yards thick, creating a network of fun ice routes that don't thaw out until spring.

Beginners head for the lower part of the valley, just west of Rjukan, where there are relatively easy routes that can be climbed in one section, on one rope. As you work your way along the valley, the climbs tend to get more difficult, culminating in the upper gorge, a confined canyon of steep, icy walls and legendary ice routes. Experts generally make a beeline for Nye Vemorkfoss, which involves scaling a near-vertical ice pillar before finishing up by the Vemork hydroelectrical plant, or head to the daunting Lipton icefall, a serious multipitch climb at the gorge's very end, on ice the color of tea. Conquering this latter route requires working in a team, navigating wafer-thin stretches and hauling yourself up over several glacial overhangs. Do this, and you'll be needing much more than just a cuppa by the time you reach the top.

Scaling one of the
hundreds of frozen
waterfalls found
in Rjukan

△ KANDERSTEG, SWITZERLAND

Test your limits—and nerves—on some of the most challenging ice routes in Europe.

Alpine Kandersteg looks beautiful in winter: a scattering of cozy chalets and mountain chapels, their wooden spires poking through the snow-laden trees. But the climbers who congregate here bypass this picturesque prospect for frozen treasures in the valleys beyond.

Within a few minutes' drive of Kandersteg is Oeschiwald, a forested area of snow-dusted pines. The cliff faces here are festooned with vertical ribbons of ice, offering an array of climbs for all levels. They make a fun starting point, despite some of the route names—Grimm, Rattenpissoir (Rat Urinal)—sounding anything but.

The real test, though, lies slightly further afield, in the icefalls of Breitwangflue. Situated above Kandersteg, this area can be reached only on skis—or, if you can get the farmer's permission, the private cable car that he uses to transport his cows to higher pastures in summer. The intrepid start is a sign of things to come: Breitwangflue is known for its challenging Water Ice routes and its highly complex Mixed Grade routes, which involve dry-tooling (using ice axes and crampons on bare rock). Among the most infamous are Crack Baby, a remarkable icefall that drops 1,115 ft (340 m), and Flying Circus, opened in 1998 by Swiss climber Robert Jasper. Expect huge stretches of daggerlike frozen formations, requiring nerves of solid steel.

Above An ice climber making their ascent of a frozen cliff face in Kandersteg

Paddling down the Gardon
river toward the stunning
arches of the Pont du Gard

Kayaking

Silently slicing across open water, propelled only by the power of a double-bladed paddle, kayaking lets you explore rivers and lakes, canals and coastlines, all from the comfort of your cockpit. Thanks to the boats' great maneuverability and stability, first-timers can easily pick up the basics and enjoy a paddle on calm waters, while more experienced kayakers can go solo, tackle white water, or cover long distances in a single day.

▷ GARDON RIVER, FRANCE

Passing beneath the Pont du Gard, this lazy stretch of the Gardon River is great for an unhurried paddle.

The Gardon River snakes from the foothills of the Cévennes Mountains, past the stone-built villages of the Gard department of Languedoc, all the way to the Mediterranean Sea. In winter, the river can transform into a torrent, but in the heat of the summer, it becomes slow-moving and shallow—perfect for a laid-back paddle. Starting from the village of Collias, you'll kayak lazily downstream for 8 km (5 miles), skimming over crystal-clear water and passing by rocky, vegetation-clad hills. It's impossible to get lost, and there's no need to rush; pull in at one of the stony beaches along the way to enjoy a languid swim or a long picnic in the sunshine. As you near the end of your trip, you'll get the chance to paddle leisurely beneath the spectacular triple-height arches of the Pont du Gard, a UNESCO-designated sight and the highest of all Roman aqueducts.

Kayaking along one of the
shady, winding waterways
in the Masurian Lakes

◁ MASURIAN LAKES, POLAND

Drift along by kayak through Poland's Lake District,
a watery world of more than 2,000 serene lakes linked
by narrow tree-lined waterways.

Masurian Lakeland (*Pojezierze Mazurskie* in Polish) is little
known to those outside of Poland and Germany. Remote and
pristine, this "land of a thousand lakes" borders Lithuania
and the Russian province of Kaliningrad, spreading out over
20,000 sq miles (52,000 sq km). Among Masuria's gentle
hills lies a riot of rivers, lakes, and wetlands, centered around
Lake Śniardwy (Poland's largest lake) and Lake Mamry (the
second largest, with several dozen island reserves). Shaped
by glaciers during the last Ice Age, this remote lake district
has changed little over the centuries, partly thanks to the
area's dense woodland, marshes, and countless lakes, which
have helped keep human impact to a minimum.

While sailing is popular on the lakes, to really explore,
you need a kayak. These small boats allow access to the
area's hidden canals and tapering rivulets, places often too
narrow to navigate in a larger vessel. Yes, there is occasional fast water where technical skill to avoid rocks and
overhanging branches is needed—on the upper sections
of the Krutynia River and the middle section of the Rospuda
River, for instance—but most of the gentle waterways and
lakes here are suitable for beginners.

Paddle down these secluded channels in the warmth of
the summer months, when the water is lazy and languid; the
slow, steady pace of your progress mirrors the cool, clear
water as the gentle current carries you onward. At points
along the thickly forested waterways, branches of oak and
conifer join overhead, creating canopies of shade for you
to glide through in glorious, silent seclusion.

As you float along, you'll have the chance to explore
the area's incredibly diverse habitats, which are made up
of UNESCO biosphere reserves and national parks. Admire
storks with their huge wingspans soaring above you, while
unruffled swans glide along next to your kayak. Many of the
birds here are migratory, and summer is a great time to spy
them. Dragonflies vibrate in the warm air and will land on
your paddle when you pause to rest, their iridescent backs
glinting in the dappled light. If you fancy a break from the
water, tie up at one of the wooden jetties or sandy beaches
to stroll the region's walking trails—Białowieża Forest and
the Biebrza Marshes have elk, deer, and beavers to discover.
Back in your kayak, keep floating downstream, watching as the
golden summer light glimmers off the water all around you.

Spotter's Guide

Great Snipe
This small, stocky wader resides
around the area's meadows and
riverside fens. It has broad wings
and a long, sharp beak to
probe in the soft mud.

Corncrake
Medium size and chestnut brown,
these birds are sometimes
streaked with buff or gray. You're
more likely to hear the male's
"krek krek" call than see this bird.

Aqautic Warbler
The Biebrza Marshes are home to
an important breeding population of this globally threatened
sandy-colored songbird. Note its
pale central crown stripe.

Cormorant
Large and dark (they look
black from a distance),
cormorants are a common
sight, often spotted standing
with their wings half open.

Gliding over the emerald waters of the spectacular Matka Gorge, surrounded by steep-sided cliffs

---
∧
Insider Tip

Most Norwegian kayak rental operators require you to show "wet card" certification *(våttkort)* to hire a kayak independently (courses are available). Less experienced kayakers can join guided adventure tours ,but sea kayaking is tough and a decent fitness is necessary.

△ MATKA GORGE, NORTH MACEDONIA

Navigate this blue-green waterway as it threads its way between the sheer walls of a scenic gorge.

Just 10 miles (16 km) from Skopje, the capital city of North Macedonia, is a liquid landscape so wildly beautiful that it's hard to believe it's man-made. Matka Gorge was created in 1938 when a dam was built on the Treska River; the rising water flooded a deep, narrow canyon, creating a winding sliver of a lake. Today, this serene waterway—the oldest artificial lake in the country—offers paddlers an easy escape from the capital. Hop in a kayak and glide over the opaque emerald waters, hemmed in by the gorge's near-vertical walls, onto whose sides determined trees cling. As you paddle, look up at the precariously perched medieval monasteries and churches, who seem to have grown from the very rock itself.

> ❝ *Hop in a kayak and glide over the opaque emerald waters, hemmed in by the gorge's near-vertical walls.* ❞

▷ TROMSØ, NORWAY

Kayak deep within Norway's Arctic Circle, over silvery seas frequented by magnificent killer whales.

Perched in the middle of an expansive sound (large sea inlet) in the far north of Norway, the island-city of Tromsø is the perfect base for a sea-kayaking adventure. The rugged coastline here offers an unbeatable backdrop for paddling: think fingerlike fjords surrounded by snowy peaks and wide sounds dotted with rugged islands. But kayakers don't just paddle here for the stunning scenery—they come for the diverse wildlife. Sea eagles and terns can often be spotted swooping above, while harbor porpoises and seals regularly glide through the icy waters, the latter often popping up unexpectedly by your boat.

The most sought-after animal to spy, however, is the *Orcinus orca*, otherwise known as the killer whale. These beautiful marine creatures (actually part of the dolphin family) migrate along this coast in winter, hunting shoals of spring-spawning herring. They can often be spotted south of Tromsø, between the islands of Kvaløya and Andøya, although (possibly because of warming seas) they have recently been glimpsed further north toward Skjervoy. Seeing pods milling and breaching the ocean's inky-blue surface is an experience never forgotten; neither is the sound of the huff of air from their blowholes, which bounces off the snow-sprinkled hills around you.

Right Killer whale emerging from the water
Far right Sea eagle soaring over the waves
Below Kayaking over calm waters at sunset

Zip-Lining

Whether you're on a humble contraption in a children's play park or a canopy tour through treetops, it's always exhilarating to whizz down a zip line. Harnessing the natural power of gravity, these aerial runways offer the combined thrill of great views and an adrenaline rush, without requiring any prior skill or training. You're spoiled for choice on locations and styles, as providers compete fiercely for the superlatives—longest, fastest, highest, and deepest.

◁ CETINA CANYON, CROATIA

Zip-line across a dramatic canyon high above the rapids of the jewel-blue Cetina River.

The Cetina River courses 62 miles (100 km) from the Dinaric Alps to the Adriatic Sea, carving a path through the rocky karst landscape of south Croatia. Close to the river mouth and the coastal town of Omiš, the narrow channel cuts deep into the riverbed and has created a gloriously scenic steep-sided canyon. It's here that adventure company Zipline Croatia has set up a series of eight steel wires for a couple of hours of adrenaline-fueled fun in the great outdoors. Altogether, more than 1 mile (2 km) of cable forms a network through the canyon, with the first six wires descending the rocky east side of the canyon wall, sometimes passing straight through its thick tree canopy and other times whistling high above it. The last two wires cross the river itself at a dizzying height of around 492 ft (150 m)—a heart-stopping finale with nothing but air between you and the water below.

Insider Tip

You don't need any special equipment for zip-lining, but it's advisable to wear long shorts or pants. The harness can make your clothes ride up when tightened, which can be uncomfortable in shorter shorts.

Gliding above the treetops amid the dramatic surrounds of Cetina Canyon in Croatia

▽ STODERZINKEN, AUSTRIA

Enjoy views of a quintessentially Alpine landscape
as you whizz below Stoderzinken mountain.

East of the Dachstein massif, Stoderzinken looms high
above the orderly Austrian town of Gröbming. In winter,
this lonely mountain peak is shrouded in snow, and a
small ski resort opens on its high slopes. For the rest of
the year, however, adrenaline seekers flock here to ride
the 1.5-mile (2.5 km) Zipline Stoderzinken, which has a
2,297 ft (700 m) drop in altitude from top to bottom.

The exhilarating journey begins with a bus transfer
along the winding Alpine road to the top station, where
staff are on hand to clip you (already snug in your
harness) onto the cable. Your heart pounds and your
breath quickens as you dangle seated at the edge of
the platform, high above the slice of valley below, in the
moments before takeoff. Stoderzinken has four parallel
zip lines, which means you and three friends can be
launched at the same time. This section—the first of
two—might be 528 ft (161 m) high, but it's fairly chilled,
and you have time to wave to your neighbors and take in
views of the pine forests and lush green scenery beneath
your feet. Not so much on the second section. This time,
the dry-mouth ride is high-adrenaline as you plummet
at up to 75 mph (120 km/h) to the final stop on an aerial
adventure that's always over far too soon.

Rocketing over the lake in
Penrhyn Quarry on the
world's fastest zip line

Zip-lining in unison above the Alpine slopes
of Stoderzinken in Austria

_____∧_____
Explore More

In the inky blackness of an
abandoned slate mine,
16 miles (25 km) inland from
Velocity 2, lies the world's
longest (427 ft/130 m) and
deepest (1,230 ft/ 375 m)
underground zip lines. Spend
a day at the Slate Caverns
(*www.zipworld.co.uk*)
adventuring in the dark,
zip-lining from one invisible
ledge to the next, in between
traverses, rappels, and an epic
leap of faith: a free-fall jump
66 ft (20 m) into the abyss.

△ SNOWDONIA, WALES

Soar over a slate mine at unimaginable speed in
the heart of Wales's adventure playground.

Snowdonia has sprung into exhilarating life in the last
decade or so. The self-appointed title of "adventure
capital of Europe" has caught on, in large part due to the
ever-increasing range of white-knuckle experiences in
the area—including an impressive network of zip lines.

As you approach Penrhyn Quarry, home to Velocity
2—the world's fastest zip line—you swiftly realize this is far
removed from the traditional zip-lining setup. Instead of
the standard seated harness, where you dangle with your
legs and arms free, here you are strapped in horizontally,
head first, with your legs tied together and arms pinned
by your sides. At a nerve-jangling 492 ft (150 m) above
the ground, Velocity 2 flings riders over the turquoise water
of the quarry lake at speeds of up to 120 mph (190 km/h).
That's faster than a skydiver's terminal velocity.

At 1 mile (1.6 km), this is the longest single zip line in
Europe, so you'll have plenty of time to take in the spectacular views—once you've gotten over the initial shock of
rocketing out of the starting point. The twinkling lake looks
peaceful underneath you, in stark contrast to the roaring
wind rushing past your ears; on a clear day, you can see to
the Isle of Man in the Irish Sea.

The leap of faith is worth it. After you've ridden Velocity 2,
other zip lines will seem like child's play.

The night sky over
La Palma, illuminated
by the ethereal form
of the Milky Way

Stargazing

Stargazing offers the chance to explore the even greater outdoors—
a ticket to boldly go on a journey to distant stars. Venture into the
remote wilds on the clearest, darkest nights and you'll be dazzled not
just by distant suns glimmering overhead but by planets and moons,
sprawling galaxies, and gossamer-like gas nebulae birthing new
stars. Even the most casual glance upward is rewarded with a
profound new sense of Earth's place in the universe.

▷ LA PALMA, CANARY ISLANDS, SPAIN

Head for the hills on the world's first Starlight Reserve
for the clearest of night skies and a celestial adventure
that's truly out of this world.

How many stars shine across the universe? Well, in truth,
nobody knows for sure. Astronomers estimate that our
own galaxy, the Milky Way, is home to some 300 billion
stars—and there are billions of galaxies. Yet most of us only
ever see the tiniest fraction of even those closest stellar
fireballs—in a city, you'll be lucky to make out a few dozen.

   Not so on the craggy volcanic speck of La Palma, the
northwesternmost of the Canary Islands. With its reliably
good weather, clear air, and minimal light pollution, this
winsome Atlantic outpost of Spain is among Europe's best
spots for stargazing. And it wants to keep things that way.
In 1988, the local government passed a "Sky Law" restricting
light, radioelectric and atmospheric pollution, even air
traffic, and in 2012 La Palma was designated the world's
first Starlight Reserve. ▶

Volcanic Origins

La Palma, it's claimed, is the world's steepest
island—and it certainly has its fair share of
slopes. Laced today by 620 miles (1,000 km) of
footpaths, the peaks, ridges and craters here
were created by millennia of volcanic activity.
The most spectacular example is the Caldera
de Taburiente, a 5-mile (8 km) wide bowl
covered in dense pine forest. But the one
scientists are watching is Cumbre Vieja, a huge
volcano in the island's south, which last erupted
in 1971—and may blow again before too long.

Spotter's Guide

Andromeda Galaxy

The closest major galaxy to Earth, a "mere" 2.5 million light-years away, is a spectacular cluster of some trillion stars in a barred spiral form.

Butterfly Cluster

Look in the constellation of Scorpius for this beautiful, butterfly-shaped cluster of some 80 stars, officially known as Messier 6.

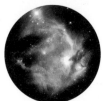

Orion Nebula

A maternity ward of stars, this vast cloud of gas and dust around 1,300 light-years from Earth lies in the "sword" hanging beneath Orion's Belt.

Albireo

View this double star through a telescope to admire the contrast between the gleaming gold star and its fainter blue twin in the constellation of Cygnus.

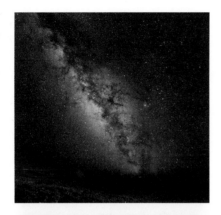

Top Looking up from the municipal
viewing point on San Antonio Volcano
Above A laser star guide beaming from
the William Herschel Telescope
at Roque de los Muchachos
Left A telescopic array at the Roque
de los Muchachos Observatory

The result is an island with not just truly dark skies but
also near-perfect conditions for the best "seeing"—an
astronomy term for the atmospheric conditions such as
temperature, air currents, weather fronts, and dust particles
that can impact on the clarity and consistency of celestial
observations. It's unsurprising, then, that the island's highest
point, Roque de los Muchachos, was chosen as the site of
an international observatory housing numerous telescopes,
including the world's largest single-aperture optical one:
the 33 ft (10 m) diameter Gran Telescopio Canarias. A
guided visit to the observatory, which is open to the public
several times weekly, is an eye-opening opportunity to learn
about the night sky and the work of the astronomers here.

You don't need such high-spec equipment to experience
the astral wonders above, though—basic binoculars or, better
still, a portable telescope, will make a big difference. Simply
venture to one of 16 municipal viewing points scattered
across the island, far from urban lighting. Each is located at
a high-altitude point for optimal stargazing and equipped
with information panels covering aspects of astronomy.

Gaze up and, as your vision adjusts, what at first seems
to be inky blackness reveals a luminous multitude of stars.
Even the naked eye will spy thousands of shining orbs,
including the gleaming veil of the Milky Way. But with the
aid of one of La Palma's expert guides, the sky really is
the limit—make out Saturn's rings or Jupiter's moons, and
perhaps a shooting star or a meteor shower. It's the closest
you'll come to traveling through space and time. Marvel
as your eyes fill with starlight emitted many millions of years
ago from constellations in the unimaginably distant cosmos.

EXMOOR NATIONAL PARK, ENGLAND

Connect with the constellations in one of England's most peaceful national parks.

Straddling the border between Somerset and Devon, Exmoor can feel remarkably remote. Away from the coast, you'll often have its heather-clad moorland and wooded valleys to yourself—which means you can enjoy the celestial show above in a kind of spiritual silence. And you're in for a real performance: constellations, star clusters, and galaxies unfolding before you in skies so richly black that Exmoor was named Europe's first International Dark Sky Reserve in 2011. Haddon Hill and Brendon Two Gates are reliable stargazing spots, or try Dunkery Beacon, the highest point in the national park, to bring you just that bit closer to the stars.

Top left Clusters of stars over a former engine house in Exmoor National Park

ZSELIC STARRY SKY PARK, HUNGARY

Spot galaxies far, far away in the forests of southern Hungary.

Trying to comprehend the distances of space is mind-boggling. Take the Triangulum Galaxy, for example, or M33 as it's also known. This spiral galaxy is 2.7 million light-years from Earth—if you set off now, you'd arrive there in roughly 54 billion years' time. But don't worry; there's no need to go that far. On a clear night, in the Zselic Starry Sky Park, you can see the galaxy with the naked eye. There are even better views of its spiral arms from the park's observatory, which is also home to a state-of-the-art planetarium. This is a great place to introduce children to the wonders of the night sky, with a program of star-watching walks through the forest.

Bottom left The cloudy clusters of the Milky Way over a lake in Zselic Starry Sky Park

TUSCANY, ITALY

Go all Galileo for the evening at an observatory in Italy's most iconic region.

Rolling hills and rows of cypress trees. Florence and the Uffizi. Pisa and its leaning tower. Fine art and fabulous food. There's so much going on at ground level in Tuscany, you'd be forgiven for forgetting to look up every now and again. But as the birthplace of Galileo, the so-called Father of Observational Astronomy, the region's night skies have played an integral part in our understanding of the universe. Southern Tuscany, in particular, offers a fabulously dark stargazing experience. To see the stars as Galileo saw them, try spying them through the telescopes at the Osservatorio di Piombino at the very tip of Punta Falcone, or the Osservatorio Polifunzionale del Chianti.

Top right The star-filled night sky above an astronomical observatory in Tuscany

WESTHAVELLAND NATURE PARK, GERMANY

Swap the bright lights of Berlin for the starry nights of lowland Brandenburg.

Where would you go to find the darkest skies in Germany? Deep into the Black Forest, perhaps, or up into the Bavarian Alps? Try a bit closer to the capital. As strange as it may seem, you need venture just 43 miles (70 km) west of Berlin to enjoy some of the best stargazing in Central Europe. With just a few small villages of half-timbered houses dotted among its marshes, the wetlands of Westhavelland Nature Park were named Germany's first International Dark Sky Reserve in 2014. The best conditions for spotting the Milky Way (regularly seen here with spine-tingling clarity) are in the reserve's "core zone," between Gülpe and Nennhausen.

Bottom right Searching for stars with a telescope in Westhavelland Nature Park

Paddling through the
Tara River Canyon in
Durmitor National Park

Whitewater Rafting

At its heart, there's an exhilarating simplicity to rafting down a river—it's about becoming one with the water, as you spin in currents, thunder down cascades, and get delightfully drenched in an inflatable boat. Rapids are graded by difficulty, with class I equaling smooth sailing and classes II to III ensuring a splashier ride. Tempted by class IV or V? You'll need rafting skills and nerves of steel.

◁ TARA RIVER, MONTENEGRO

Revel in the might of the Tara River on an exhilarating voyage through Europe's deepest canyon.

The Tara River flows across Montenegro, snaking 91 miles (146 km) from the rugged Komovi Mountains in the southeast to the border with Bosnia and Herzegovina in the northwest. Fed en route by numerous springs and tributaries, the river's waters become increasingly powerful over the course of its descent, forming dozens of roaring cascades and churning rapids.

This in itself would be reason enough to reach for your paddle, but the Tara gets even better as it picks up pace. The latter half of its length weaves through the craggy splendor of the 48-mile (78 km) Tara River Canyon,

the deepest canyon in Europe at a dizzying 4,265 ft (1,300 m)—and the second deepest in the world, after the US's Grand Canyon.

It's here in the canyon that the majority of whitewater rafting trips on the Tara take place, right in the heart of Durmitor National Park. The river threads through this primeval setting like a teal ribbon, dancing past banks cloaked with old-growth black pine trees, under the steadfast gaze of the snow-streaked mountains that loom above. Class III and IV rapids send boats careening down cascades and spinning in the currents, requiring you to summon all your strength to navigate the torrent, tilting oars to swerve around rocks, and occasionally hunkering down, allowing the Tara's foamy crests to propel you along. At journey's end, rafters disembark exhausted, with hearts thudding, eager to do it all over again tomorrow.

Navigating the choppy
waters of the Noce River
in the Val di Sole

◁ NOCE RIVER, ITALY

Brave the rapids on this daredevil river-run
in the shadow of the Dolomites.

Simply put, the Noce is the most adventurous whitewater
rafting river in Europe. Rising among the peaks of northern
Italy, it drifts, tumbles, and then rages its way down through
the Val di Sole (Sun Valley) in the Dolomites. The 17-mile
(28 km) stretch that's navigable by raft is a pure adrenaline
rush of rocks and froth. There's just enough time to soak
up your mountainous surroundings before your raft starts
bouncing its way along the chilly turquoise waters, with
trees crowding the banks on both sides as you descend
through the valley. There are several fearsome rapids to
navigate until—with the river's speed increasing and the
hillsides closing in—you can pull out at Ponti Stori and
pause to get your breath back.

> ❝ *The 17-mile (28 km)
> stretch that's navigable by
> raft is a pure adrenaline
> rush of rocks and froth.* ❞

▽ DRANSE RIVER, FRANCE

Savor stirring views and gentle thrills on the
babbling waters of the Dranse.

The Dranse River originates high in the Chablais Alps,
gushing from the confluence of three different waterways.
Its icy-cold torrents snake for a scenic 30 miles (49 km)
down to Lac Léman (Lake Geneva). The river's name is
said to stem from a Celtic term for "fast running, violent
water," and for centuries its currents provided power to
local sawmills. Nowadays, however, the Dranse's flow is
controlled by a hydroelectric dam, which makes its course
much more predictable—and therefore ideal for first-time
rafters and those seeking to experience the river *en famille*.

The river's moderate meander lets rafters quickly
settle into a steady rhythm—paddling past wooden chalets,
ducking overhanging trees, and marveling at the huge
boulders and sheer cliffs that line the banks. This idyllic
corner of the Haute-Savoie is an important habitat for
wildlife, and there's ample opportunity between rapids
to spot leaping fish and dams built by resident beavers.
You might also spy a few fellow adventurers as you drift
downriver—the Dranse is a popular location for whitewater
swimming and canyoning.

This may not be a full-on white-knuckle ride, but it's not
without thrills—expect a heavy-duty soaking of spray on
the bumpy Escalier (Stairs) section, as you navigate a series
of drops through the river's whirling eddies. Even the
calmer stretches bring their own drama, with optional
riverside cliff jumps—nothing gets the blood pumping quite
like leaping from a 23 ft (7 m) high rocky shelf into the
refreshingly cool embrace of the water.

Healing Waters

The crystal-clear waters of the Dranse have
long had a reputation for healing. Swanky
Évian-les-Bains, on the shore of Lac Léman, has
been a wellness destination ever since France's
19th-century spa heyday, along with Thonon-
les-Bains to its west. Locals swear the benefits
are enormous, whether you imbibe the waters
or soak in them. Bring a bottle to fill, or book
a *cure thermale* (spa treatment) to feel the
full restorative effects.

Steering through
a whitewater rapid
on the Dranse

Hut-to-Hut Hiking

Wake in a rustic cabin, munch breakfast alongside fellow trekkers, lace up your boots, and head out on an unfamiliar stretch of path. Arrive at your next berth, share stories over dinner, bed down in a cozy dorm. Then repeat, day after glorious day. This mesmerizing rhythm is one of the great joys of hut-to-hut hiking along Europe's long-distance trails, yet it's far from repetitive. Each morning brings fresh views, each habitat different wildlife, each evening new friends, each mile a renewed sense of achievement. It's the most rewarding way to get from A to B (and on to C, D, and E).

◁ LAUGAVEGUR TRAIL, ICELAND

Traverse candy-striped rhyolite mountains, dramatic lava fields, and eerie rock formations on this classic trail across Iceland's wild uplands.

This spectacular route's name translates as "Hot Spring Road"—and while that's certainly accurate (you'll cross steaming and gurgling geothermal fields), it's far from the whole picture. Indeed, the diversity of landscapes you'll encounter along this 34-mile (54 km) waymarked trail is what's made this the country's most popular trekking route.

Snaking between Landmannalaugar and Þórsmörk in southwest Iceland, Laugavegur is not to be taken lightly. Reaching the trailhead requires a 4WD, and you'll need to carry food supplies and be ready to wade across icy rivers. ▶

Striking, multicolored
scenery along Iceland's
Laugavegur Trail

⌃

Explore More

Though many trekkers set out
immediately on arriving at
Landmannalaugar and catch
the bus back to Reykjavík
from Þórsmörk, it's well worth
adding on days at either end
of the hike to explore more of
these wild landscapes. From
Landmannalaugar, roam the
trails lacing Fjallabak Nature
Reserve, and from Þórsmörk,
consider continuing along
the two-day trek to Skógar,
between Mýrdalsjökull and
Eyjafjallajökull glaciers.

Weather changes rapidly in these highlands, which top
3,937 ft (1,200 m)—fog can descend and snow can fall
at any time. But for experienced walkers, it's a relatively
accessible and compact two- to four-day hike, rewarding
with ample scenic grandeur.

Expect to be dazzled from the off. Just south of the start
at Landmannalaugar, you'll walk between steaming hot
springs, across glinting black lava fields, and beneath the
rainbow rhyolite ridges and gorges of Brennisteinsalda. You'll
then reach the spurting geyser at Stórihver and, finally, your
first hut, Höskuldsskáli. And that's just the start: on subse-
quent days, you'll encounter rocky canyons, snow-dusted
peaks, and creaking ice caps. You might recognize one of
the latter: the ice cap Eyjafjallajökull sits atop its namesake
volcano, whose 2010 eruption caused global travel chaos.

Your final destination is suitably magical: Þórsmörk,
named for the Norse thunder god Thor. This verdant region
of glacial streams, weird rock formations, and—a rarity in
Iceland—birch woods provides a fittingly legendary end
to a truly otherworldly odyssey.

The Höskuldsskáli hut in
Hrafntinnusker, the first
stop along the trail

Hiking over a small bridge in remote Swedish countryside on the Kungsleden Trail

△ KUNGSLEDEN TRAIL, SWEDEN

Meet reindeer and Sami herders along the "King's Trail," which winds through the Arctic wilderness of Swedish Lapland.

Summer in far northern Sweden heralds endless days (from late May to mid-July, the sun never sets above the Arctic Circle) and is the perfect season for hiking the mountains, birch forests, lakes, and glacial valleys of this wild, remote landscape. The Kungsleden, Sweden's most famous trail, stretches over 250 miles (400 km) south from Abisko, near the northern border with Norway, to Hemavan. Developed over a number of years from the late 19th century, the route traverses no fewer than three national parks, as well as the lands of the indigenous Sami people; you'll likely encounter their reindeer herds en route. The northern section in particular is studded with cozy cabins, most stocked with food supplies, making the 65-mile (105 km) stretch between Abisko and Nikkaluokta a dream for first-timer hut-to-hutters.

" *The northern section in particular is studded with cozy mountain cabins, most stocked with food supplies.* "

Standing at the top of Colle Santu Petru, a mountain pass on the GR20 across Corsica

▷ GR20 TRAIL, CORSICA

Trace the rugged spine of the "mountain in the sea" on a challenging trek through wild scrub and plunging valleys.

Politically a region of France but spiritually a land apart, Corsica has a soul as tough and dramatic as its landscapes—and as the trail rated by many as Europe's most demanding long-distance trek. The Grande Randonée (GR) 20 snakes 112 miles (180 km) southeast from Calenzana to Conca, along the backbone of this spectacular Mediterranean island. Over 16 stages, you'll plunge through dense, aromatic maquis (scrub), along vertiginous ridges, down into deep valleys, and over lofty cols. And each night, you'll bed down in a mountain refuge alongside fellow trekkers, sharing tales of the day's travails.

There's a reason that the GR20 has a somewhat fearsome reputation. Long, steep ascents and descents soon add up, and weather is notoriously fickle at higher altitudes. You'll need to carry most supplies—the nearest shops are typically serious detours from the trail—and ideally a tent, in case refuges are full. And some sections take nerve as well as stamina, with fixed chains traversing sheer rock faces.

Yet the payback is immense. You'll trek through fragrant, boar-snuffled pinewoods, stark granite rock-scapes, and boggy marshland, passing glittering glacial lakes and snowcapped peaks where you might spy soaring lammergeier or grazing mouflon. And by the time you descend into Conca, near the glorious beaches of the southeast, you'll truly understand the Corsican name for the GR20: Fra li Monti—Across the Mountains.

Mountain Shepherds

The GR20 strings together some of the countless ancient footpaths forged by Corsica's shepherds. For centuries, families drove their flocks from winter grazing near the coast up to summer pastures in the mountains, where they tended and milked the animals to make the strong-smelling cheese for which Corsica is famed. Today, just a few hardy souls continue this traditional lifestyle, but you might still pick up pungent *fromage corse* at a few of the old dry-stone cottages along the trail.

Spotter's Guide

Mouflon

Mouflon are thought to be the ancestors of domestic sheep. Once hunted almost to extinction in Corsica, they are now a protected species.

Wild Boar

Covered with dark, bristly fur, wild boar feed on chestnuts, acorns, and truffles. They are hunted for their meat, which is a local delicacy.

Corsican Nuthatch

The tiny Corsican nuthatch is the only endemic bird in France. It inhabits the mountain forests of the island's interior and likes to nest in old laricio pines.

Laricio Pine

Endemic to Corsica, the laricio pine is a large coniferous evergreen tree that can reach a height of 131 ft (40 m) and live for up to 500 years.

Kiteboarding

Kiteboarding—also known as kitesurfing—is a contradiction: wild yet calming, complicated yet elegantly simple. Harnessing the power of the wind using a large kite, you'll glide across the water with your feet strapped loosely to a board. The hours of dedication spent mastering this sport are exponentially rewarding, and the intense rush felt when first standing up on the board just gets sweeter as you progress—as does the freeing feeling of riding on the open ocean.

Riding over the shimmering waters of Óbidos Lagoon, surrounded by stunning coastal views

◁ ÓBIDOS, PORTUGAL

A stunning backdrop, year-round wind, no crowds, and a choice of butter-flat shallow water or roaring waves—Óbidos has everything a kiteboarder could ever ask for.

The sandy shores of the Algarve, Portugal's southernmost region, remain the country's attention-grabbing tourist magnet. But head north to the Silver Coast, and you'll swiftly leave the crowds behind. This peaceful area—which gets its name from the effect of the sun's reflection sparkling off the Atlantic waves—is a haven of rugged coastlines and expansive beaches, not to mention some excellent kiteboarding spots.

The best of these is to be found at Óbidos, a charming medieval town made up of winding cobbled streets that burst with blooming bougainvillea. The town itself is situated inland, but the Atlantic coast to its immediate northwest is home to the glittering expanse of the Óbidos Lagoon, the largest saltwater lagoon in Europe. The coast here is prime kiteboarding territory, with mild temperatures and consistent winds. There's also the added bonus that, as it's still refreshingly undeveloped, it never draws the large crowds of more established resorts—so you can have the lagoon (almost) to yourself. ▶

Top Practicing jumps
in Óbidos Lagoon
Above Carving through
the calm waters
Right Kiteboarding in
the lagoon at sunset

The Wedding Town

The town of Óbidos has an unusual history; it was once a traditional wedding present from Portuguese kings to their new wives. The custom began in the 13th century, when King Dinis showed the town to his fiancée Dona Isabel (aged just 10); it so entranced her that he decided to include it in her dowry. The tradition continued for another 600 years or so, leading Óbidos to be nicknamed "The Wedding Town."

The flat, shallow water of the lagoon is great for learning the basics. Crisscrossing up and down the turquoise expanse is a relatively gentle experience, bringing views of golden sandbars against a backdrop of lush, green hills dotted with white-washed houses. Your feet will never be far from the bottom in the waist-high water, so if you come out of your bindings and lose your board—highly likely if you're still getting the hang of the sport—then you can get back to it with relative ease. And in these controlled conditions, you may find that you can progress quickly to trying more technical moves and jumps.

Once you've mastered the sport, it's possible to explore beyond the sheltered waters of the lagoon. At high tide, more experienced kiteboarders ride away from the flat shallows to play in the choppy waves of the open Atlantic Ocean. Out here, as the wind whips the cresting water and the salty air hits your nostrils, you're greeted with views of the golden cliffs that sweep down the south side of the beach at the lagoon's entrance. If you were to design the ideal kiteboarding spot, this would surely be it.

TARIFA, SPAIN

Experience world-class conditions at
Europe's windy kiteboarding mecca.

Legend has it that the wind in Tarifa is so
powerful it drives residents insane. True or not,
it's undeniable that the wind is all-consuming,
blowing almost nonstop year-round—with such
conditions, it's unsurprising that the city has
become the kiteboarding capital of Europe.
Lying at the meeting point of the Atlantic and
the Mediterranean, Tarifa's shores are dominated
by two winds that alternate throughout the
year. The Poniente is the one for kiteboarders
still building their skills—warm, 15–25 knots, and
blowing toward or parallel to the shore. The
easterly Levante is much stronger (20–40 knots)
and often gusts out to sea, creating choppy
conditions that only experts can handle.

Top left Harnessing Tarifa's powerful wind on an
expert-level binding-free surfboard

PISSOURI, CYPRUS

Warm, flat water; consistent winds; and no
crowds—Pissouri is perfect for learners.

First-time kiteboarder? Pissouri, in southwest
Cyprus, is an ideal place to learn in peace.
Neither the curved pebble beach nor the sparkling azure waters of the bay get busy here—
meaning there's a lot of room to launch your
kite and even more room to maneuver once
you're out on the water. The bay is also
sheltered enough to keep the water calm but
has plenty of consistent—and relatively gentle—
wind to enable riders to develop their abilities.
The first time you get up on the board is a rush
you won't forget—one minute you're struggling
to get your balance while trying to maneuver
the kite, then all of a sudden you're speeding
over the water as though you're lighter than air.

Bottom left Riding the crowd-free, deep-blue waters
found off the coast of Cyprus

LIEPĀJA, LATVIA

Progress your riding skills alongside
the locals on the waters of the Baltic.

Liepāja, on Latvia's west coast, is known as the
"City of Wind"—the kind of moniker that eager
kiteboarders can't easily ignore. The steady wind
that blows here rarely gets above 15 knots, so it
makes a particularly good destination for fledg-
ling kiteboarders to learn the ropes. Even better,
just off Liepāja beach is a specially designated
kiteboarding zone where you can practice your
wave riding. Beginners here have an added
motivation to quickly learn to balance on their
boards, too—after all, the Baltic Sea isn't famed
for its warmth. Once you've got the hang of
things, make for the main beach—an idyllic
5-mile (8 km) stretch of ultra-fine white sand
backed by forest—to continue refining your skills.

Top right Kiteboarding over the Baltic Sea, just off
the beautiful sands of Liepāja beach

SANKT PETER-ORDING, GERMANY

Ride gnarly waves and practice tricks on flat
lagoons at this world-class kiteboarding spot.

Having hosted 10 Kitesurf World Cups, Sankt
Peter-Ording is the place to emulate the pros
on world-beating waves. Here, sand dunes and
salt meadows are punctuated by the country's
biggest beach, which stretches for 7 miles
(12 km)—that size means there's some great
variety for kiteboarding. Hauptstrand, the central
stretch of beach, has wild waves, which can
reach up to 13 ft (4 m)—they're particularly
strong out toward the reef at high tide. To the
south, Südstrand is a shallow lagoon, sheltered by
a sandbank, with flat conditions perfect for practicing freestyle tricks. Wherever you go, you'll be
giving the pros a run for their money in no time.

Bottom right Group of kiteboarders skimming over
the waves at Sankt Peter-Ording in Germany

Via Ferrata

Reaching the heady heights of a mountain can seem intimidating if you don't have climbing experience, but via ferrata (meaning "iron path" in Italian) makes some of Europe's best climbing spots more accessible. Created from iron rungs, ladders, bridges, and pegs, plus cabling that you can clip yourself onto for safety, these set routes (and the company of a local guide) allow you to take part in exposed and otherwise technical climbs.

▷ DOLOMITES, ITALY

Explore the remote peaks of Italy's ruggedly beautiful Dolomites on this challenging multiday via ferrata route.

The Dolomites are blessed with more than 150 incredible via ferrata routes, which crisscross the region's craggy granite mountains. The first of these "iron paths" were laid during World War I, as Italian and Austrian troops engaged in fierce battles high in the mountains. Today, thousands of adrenaline–fueled mountain lovers head here every year to get a taste of true mountaineering and to experience up close the sheer scale and majesty of the saw-toothed peaks that dominate the skyline. There's something to satisfy every level, from short, relatively straightforward climbs to much more technical routes. ▶

Insider Tip

All beginners should employ a professional guide who can explain the basics of via ferrata and provide assistance on trickier sections. Experienced climbers can use their own equipment to go it alone, although local guides can still be useful to help show you the quieter routes away from the crowds.

Clambering along rock faces with epic views in the Dolomites

A Dark Past

The "iron paths" that today provide thrilling adventures in the Dolomites were not made for recreation. In fact, the via ferrata here were laid by opposing Italian and Austrian troops during World War I to help establish summit bases, from where each side fought to maintain control of the high ground. The Italians called this region *il fronte verticale* (the vertical front). As many as 60,000 troops are said to have died in avalanches in the Dolomites during the war.

For a particularly daring challenge, try tackling the untamed Giro de Sorapiss. This epic circuit takes you on a thrilling two-day adventure among some of the region's most remote peaks. Spanning three separate via ferratas—the Alfonso Vandelli, Sentiero Carlo Minazio, and Francesco Berti—the route crosses some truly testing terrain. Expect to clamber up craggy, vertigo-inducing mountainsides, shuffle along precipitous narrow ledges (where you'll be strapped onto sturdy cables attached to the rock face), and crawl down near-vertical cliff faces via strong iron ladders. On the way, you'll stay in simple *refugios* (mountain huts), perched near vivid blue lakes, or surrounded by pines and peaks; you'll also take in the blistering views of undulating forested valleys, from which emerge the region's iconic sky-scraping peaks. As the sun reflects off the pale rock faces, be sure to take some time to pause and enjoy a deep breath of fresh mountain air as the adrenaline rush slowly subsides.

Right Traversing an exposed section of rock
Below Climber scrambling along a ledge attached to a strong cable

▽ MAROKKA, AUSTRIA

This accessible via ferrata promises gorgeous Tyrolean vistas for those with less climbing experience.

Adventurous families and those reasonably new to climbing can enjoy a gentler introduction to the world of via ferrata on this guided route to the summit of Marokka, overlooking the Wildsee in Austria's Tyrolean Mountains. It's not for total beginners—this route is rated B/C, with A being the easiest and E the hardest—but if you're fit and have some climbing experience, then it's a fantastic place to get familiar with the ins and outs of the iron way. The two-hour climb begins at the Fieberbrunn cable-car station and takes in exciting scrambles and grassy paths atop mountain ridges en route to the summit. Despite not being an especially challenging ascent, it still packs in some heart-in-the-mouth thrills—not least the crossing of a rudimentary rope bridge that sways unnervingly with every step.

Above Walking across the rope bridge on the Marokka via ferrata in Austria's Tyrolean Mountains

> *"Whichever route you take, this vertigo-inducing climb is a challenge."*

◁ JULIAN ALPS, SLOVENIA

Ascend Slovenia's highest peak in the rugged, high ridges of the Julian Alps.

Sweeping from northeast Italy into Slovenia, the Julian Alps are characterized by high ridges made of tall, snow-capped peaks. The undisputed king of them all is Triglav. Found within the eponymous national park, this mountain is both a cultural icon—it appears on the country's flag—and Slovenia's tallest peak at 9,396 ft (2,864 m) high.

Three via ferrata routes—Tominšek, Bamberglead, and Čez Prag—lead up to Triglav's soaring summit from Vrata Valley, ascending the mountain via its steep north face. Whichever route you take, this vertigo-inducing climb is a challenge; it usually needs two days and involves taxing ascents up near-vertical wall faces and a walk along a knife-edge ridgeline, complete with sheer drops on each side. The effort required is both physical and mental, but you'll be rewarded with some truly spectacular views on the way, including sky-blue rivers, Alpine forests, and, from the summit, rows of iron-gray peaks that stretch into the distance.

Scaling a steep slope
on Mount Triglav in
Slovenia's Julian Alps

Navigating the rocky Pembrokeshire coastline on a coasteering trip

Coasteering

There's a childlike joy to coasteering—a combination of swimming and scrambling, cliff jumping and walking along a stretch of coastline. Mixing adventurous play with immersion in the seascape, it involves swimming through natural arches, scampering up rocky ledges, and leaping into deep pools. While the expert could go it alone, typically you'd book with a local outdoor instructor who has tested the route, knows the tide times, and provides wet suits, helmets, and buoyancy aids.

◁ PEMBROKESHIRE COAST NATIONAL PARK, WALES

Head to the birthplace of coasteering to clamber over ancient cliffs, dive into the Atlantic, and immerse yourself in a wild coastal landscape.

There's nowhere in Europe that can rival Pembrokeshire, a Welsh county famed for its coastal national park, for coasteering. The activity was born here over 30 years ago, when Andy Middleton—a savvy outdoor instructor from St. Davids in North Pembrokeshire—started offering guided excursions of the area's rugged coastline through his company TYF. By the mid-1990s, coasteering's popularity had begun to boom, and today this adventurous activity is recognized, practiced, and celebrated around the world. ▶

Top A stretch of
stunning coastline
south of St. Davids
Above Enjoying a
dip in the sea

Spotter's Guide

Atlantic Grey Seal

Look out for the glistening
flanks of these doglike
creatures. Their coats vary from
silvery-gray to brown, often
including blotches.

Chough

Britain's rarest crow is a regular
on the Pembrokeshire coast. It
has glossy black plumage,
a jaunty red bill and legs, and
a "chee-ow" call.

Snakelocks Anemone

Found in rock pools, these squat
brown creatures use their long,
beautiful green and purple
tentacles to capture prey such
as prawns and sea snails.

Spider Crabs

These long-armed crabs are
commonly spotted between
June and August, when they
pile up in mounds, shed their
shells, and mate.

Jumping into the
chilly waters of
the Atlantic

Blue-Rayed Limpet

Look out for these fingernail-
sized mollusks clinging to kelp
fronds. When light hits their
neon-blue stripes, they reflect
a brilliant fluorescent flash.

Pembrokeshire's seascape could have been designed specifically for coasteering. The variety of rock formations along its rugged coastline means there's always a new challenge around the corner. Expect craggy coves to clamber along, rocky gullies to negotiate, hidden sea caves to explore, and staggering cliffs to climb. One minute you could be traversing a slippery length of shore, sea spray whipping your face, and the next jumping from a high ledge straight into the Atlantic—the water might be chilly, but, thanks to your warming wet suit, you won't feel the cold. All you need to give coasteering here a go is an expert guide, an appetite for adventure, and the desire to get absolutely soaked.

There are plenty of amazing spots to try out coasteering here; in fact, guides often use different sites depending on the conditions. One excellent spot is St. Non's Bay, tucked below a ruined chapel that marks the birthplace of Wales's patron saint, St. David. Here, you can hop across rocky outcrops, scramble alongside ridged cliffs, and fling yourself into the deep, sapphire waters. Watch for wildlife as you go—negotiate barnacle-encrusted footholds, glimpse vibrant sea anemones, and watch as rare choughs perform acrobatic swoops above you. If you're lucky, you might meet a curious seal or spot a dolphin further out to sea; both of these marine animals thrive in the nutrient-rich waters that surround the Pembrokeshire coastline.

Another great location is the stretch of shoreline near Abereiddy Beach. Scramble along the coast, keeping an eye out for fossils—the cliffs here are more than 500 million years old—and fling yourself into the rippling water to body surf in the swell. There's also the chance to slide down rocky flumes pounded by frothing surf and take a heart-pounding 33 ft (10 m) leap into the Blue Lagoon, a sea-flooded slate quarry. Afterward, warmed by a cozy jacket and that post-adventure afterglow, you'll stand on the clifftops and gaze out to sea, imagining what the next day will bring.

◁ ARRÁBIDA NATURAL PARK, PORTUGAL

In this glorious yet accessible paradise, coasteering includes added action-hero dimensions.

Despite lying just 31 miles (50 km) from Lisbon, Arrábida Natural Park feels like a far-flung Mediterranean utopia. Wooded hills drop off to chalky limestone cliffs, footed by frills of white coves and lapped by a glassy jade sea.

While the scenery here may be serene, the coasteering is far from it. Most guided trips start as they mean to go on, with a thrilling jet-boat ride to one of the secluded locations along the craggy shore. From here, the usual scrambling, swimming, and cliff-jumping that coasteering is known for is combined with added adrenaline-pumping activities—think short sections of roped climbing up rugged rocks and rappelling down wave-slapped cliffs. Best of all, you'll even get the chance to zoom via a fast-and-furious zip line straight into the sparkling sea.

> " *While the scenery here may be serene, the coasteering is far from it.* "

Zip-lining into teal-colored waters off the coast of Arrábida Natural Park

△ CONNEMARA, IRELAND

Submerge yourself in the rugged beauty of Ireland's wild west coast.

Hidden in the northwest corner of County Galway, Connemara's coastline is simply stunning. The tweedy colors of heather, bog, granite, and grass that dominate the area's landscape transform as you approach the coast, giving way to white-sand beaches and cobalt waters that are almost Caribbean-like in their vibrancy. Coasteering here will take you across these sugary sweeps of sand and plunge you into the crystal-clear—but nevertheless chilly—sea. Clambering over rough rock, you'll explore an untamed landscape of rarely seen bays and caves, elegant arches, deep gullies, and soaring sea stacks, all formed by the persistent wild beating of the Atlantic Ocean against the coast's soft sandstone.

Looking over the rugged coastline of Connemara, on Ireland's west coast

▷ TYROL, AUSTRIA

The snow-blanketed valleys and slopes of Tyrol are pure heaven for snowshoers, thanks to the hundreds of easily accessible trails that crisscross the region.

Tucked away in the Austrian Alps, Tyrol is best known as a skiing and snowboarding paradise come winter. But these aren't the only ways to explore this snow-blanketed region—cutting through the landscape are more than 500 well-marked snowshoeing trails, many opening up otherwise impassable areas to curious explorers. Here, your biggest dilemma each day will be deciding which route to take through the shimmering, snow-bound landscapes.

   Some of the best routes are found in Tyrol's Hohe Tauern National Park, the largest protected area in the Alps, which transforms into a frozen utopia during the snowy winter months. Strap on your snowshoes and slide past hulking blue-tinged glaciers, skirt the edge of glittering frozen lakes, or tread through virgin snow around the base of Großglockner, Tyrol's highest peak at 12,460 ft (3,798 m).

Above Snowshoes propped up in the snow
Right Hiking through the frosted landscapes of Tyrol

Snowshoeing

Snowshoeing—moving through snowy landscapes, enabled
by wide, racketlike footwear—allows you to explore otherwise
inaccessible wintry realms, often without another soul in sight.
With snowflakes falling and a chill to the air, you'll tread
peacefully through spectacular frosted wonderlands, with only
the sound of your footsteps to disturb the serenity of the moment.
Simply grab some warm gear and walking poles, strap on a
pair of snowshoes, and set off with a sense of adventure.

Cutting tracks through fresh powder in the Apuseni Mountains

△ TRANSYLVANIA, ROMANIA

Explore the untamed landscapes and geological secrets of Romania's remote Apuseni Mountains.

Tucked away in the northwest corner of Transylvania, the little-visited Apuseni Mountains are wonderfully wild. Here, accompanied by an expert guide, you can sculpt fresh tracks through gently rolling snowy valleys and swoosh through silent glades surrounded by frosted spruce and mountain beech. You can even scale some of the area's undulating summits, including Cucurbăta Mare, the highest peak in the Apuseni range at 6,066 ft (1,849 m).

But snowshoeing here is as much about what's beneath the powder as above it. The park has some amazing geological formations—formed over millennia by the erosion of its soft limestone—many of which can be found along snowshoeing routes. Highlights include the spectacular caverns of Vartop, dotted with impressive stalagmites and stalactites, and the exquisite ice formations of Scărișoara, a huge cave home to Europe's largest underground glacier.

" *Swoosh through silent glades surrounded by frosted spruce and mountain beech.* "

▷ MERCANTOUR NATIONAL PARK, FRANCE

Journey through snow-encased mountain landscapes into the heart of this national park.

Nestled in the south of the French Alps, Mercantour National Park stretches along the mountainous Italian border for almost 62 miles (100 km). A handful of small, chocolate-box villages dot the park's periphery, but its interior—made up of six sweeping valleys encircled by piercing peaks—is uninhabited. The park feels especially rugged and untamed in winter, when the forests and mountains are cloaked in white icing. But once you're armed with *raquettes* (snowshoes), it's surprisingly easy to explore, thanks to the selection of trails that snake their way through the sparkling snowy landscape.

Don't worry if you're still finding your feet with snowshoeing, as there are routes here for all abilities. Nestled in a sloping valley near the Italian border, the red-roofed village of Saint-Étienne-de-Tinée is ideal for beginners or families, with mountains on your doorstep and amenities a stone's throw away. Head off on your own to explore the networks of easily accessible, signposted trails, which take you through snow-bowed evergreen forests, past ice-clad waterfalls, and along low-lying mountain passes, around which loom jagged peaks. Even more remote valleys, tucked away deep within the park and dotted with wildlife tracks, can be uncovered by beginners on a guided trip.

Experienced snowshoers, meanwhile, will relish the village of Estenc, located right in the midst of the park and often disguised under blankets of snow. After a night in a snow-crusted gîte or a traditional wooden-beamed chalet, you can strap on your snowshoes and circle nearby 9,840 ft (3,000 m) peaks right from your front door. Not to be missed is the tough, day-long trail from Estenc to the frozen Lac d'Allos, Europe's biggest natural high-mountain lake, set within a crater of dizzying peaks. It's prime territory to spot curved-horned ibex observing you from the

Rock Ptarmigan

Part of the grouse family, these crow-sized game birds turn completely white in winter.

Ibex

Iconic to the French Alps, Ibex are recognized by their distinctive long and curved horns.

Golden Eagle

This large bird of prey is famed for its vast wingspan, hunting prowess and mythical reputation.

Chamois

Marvellus climbers, these goat-like animals can dislodge rocks on the ridges, so pass by with caution.

slopes above or rock ptarmigan perched on the snow nearby; if you're really lucky, you might even spot an alpine hare, its white fur providing perfect camouflage in the pristine snow.

For those seeking to explore the farthest reaches of the park, mountain refuges offer an unforgettable experience. These picturesque Alpine shelters—typically stone-walled or wood-framed—perch in high mountain locations and allow you to snowshoe from hut to hut on multiday adventures. Each morning, you'll wake above the clouds, then step outside to feel the biting Alpine air upon your skin and take in panoramic mountain views. In the south of Mercantour, a number of these huts are found close to the Italian border. With either plenty of experience or a guide, you can use these refuges to spend several days touring the slopes of Cime du Gélas, the highest peak in the park at 10,312 ft (3,143 m). Here, with the landscape encased in an icy winter grip and birds of prey swooping elegantly overhead, the raw power of the Alps is undeniable.

Snowshoeing in Mercantour National Park

Woodland Foraging

Creating a sense of connection with your hunter-gatherer forebears, if only for a moment, foraging among forests and hedgerows is a rewarding antidote to rushed urban living. Follow the simple rules of not breaking roots or branches and leaving plenty behind for others, and you'll soon find you have a feast of fresh, wild ingredients without a plastic packet in sight.

Top A *trifolao* and his dog in search of truffles
Bottom left A freshly dug truffle
Bottom right "White diamonds" prepared for cooking

◁ PIEDMONT, ITALY

Tour the woodlands of Piedmont to discover the "white diamond"—a truffle that's renowned for being one of the world's most expensive ingredients.

The Piedmont region of Italy knows how to celebrate its culinary culture, with frequent festivals and a deep-rooted emphasis on slow living and fine foods—many of which can be found in the woods and rolling vineyards here. One of the most sought-after delicacies is the white truffle, or *tartufo bianco*, which grows only from September to January, a few inches beneath the leaf-strewn forest floor. Join a tour with a local *trifolao* (truffle hunter) and their dog to sniff out these local treasures, the best of which are smooth, hard to the touch, and the size of a golf ball. The surrounding trees of oak, hazelnut, poplar, willow, and chestnut all feed into the truffles' earthy aroma, which is also infused with notes of garlic, honey, hay, and spices.

The Edible Country

Inspired by the Nordic food movement, where Scandinavian chefs plate up exquisite dishes of foraged foods and flowers, Visit Sweden *(www.visitsweden.com)* has placed special picnic tables in wild locations around the country. Foragers who reserve a spot via the online system can pick, cook, and eat foods from their stunning natural surroundings, following seasonal menus devised by Michelin-starred chefs. What better way to end a day of foraging than by dishing up the freshest and most seasonal of meals?

Picking ripe bilberries from a shrub in the forest

Spotter's Guide

Lingonberry

Bright red lingonberries come from the same family as cranberries and share a similar taste. They're often used to make jam.

Bilberry

Found on small, oval-leaved shrubs, bilberries have traditionally been used to treat a variety of medical problems, particularly eye ailments.

Wild Strawberry

Much smaller than their commercial counterparts, these tiny fruits are hard to spot but can be found on bushes in the forest in June and July.

Cloudberry

Also known as yellowberries, salmonberries, and bakeapples, these amber fruits grow in boggy areas and are highly prized by foragers.

Scouring shrubs
on the forest floor
in search of berries

◁ ORMANÄS FOREST, SWEDEN

Hike into Sweden's natural pantry armed with
a wicker basket and a keen eye to gather the
fruits of the forest.

Sweden is a forager's dream. The ancient principle
of Allemansrätten, "every man's right," allows people
to roam the countryside freely, providing they respect
the landscape. Plus, more than half of Sweden is
covered by uninhabited forest, so living off the
bounty of the land is ingrained in the culture here.

Ormanäs Forest lies at the southernmost tip of
the country. Here, you can gaze at the calm lakes
amid the majestic beech trees and scour low-lying
shrubs for morsels. The region is known for its
berries, particularly bilberries, which are rumored
to enhance night vision. Similar to blueberries,
bilberries are almost black when ripe, with a dusty-
gray coating and purple-red juice that will stain
your fingers. When eaten raw, they are slightly bitter,
but they become much sweeter when cooked—try
them in *blåbärspaj*, Swedish bilberry pie.

Not far from the bilberry bush, you'll likely spot
the foliage of antioxidant-packed lingonberries.
In springtime, the shrubs display small, pink-white
flowers hanging like delicate bells. The red fruits
follow in summer and have an acidic taste, but if
you can wait until fall, these round, pea-sized
berries will be far sweeter.

Another summer bloomer is the cloudberry, but
you'll have to be quick to catch them in season. For
just a few weeks each year, these golden-orange
berries burst from thornless shrubs that creep
across the forest floor. Like a small raspberry in
shape, each fruit sits at the end of a short stalk.
Pop one in your mouth for a fresh, sour taste and a
hit of vitamin C. With such an abundance of natural
goodies, no wonder Sweden is consistently ranked
among the happiest countries in the world.

" *Soft, mossy verges become speckled with white, yellow, brown, black, and even purple toadstools.* "

▷ BLACK FOREST, GERMANY

Spend a crisp fall day scavenging the forest floor of this fairy-tale woodland for edible fungi.

With its wood-clad buildings, red spotted toadstools, and streams winding around mossy boulders, the Black Forest certainly comes with fairy-tale charm. It was so named for the thickness of the canopy, which historically let in very little light—it's easy to picture Hansel and Gretel getting lost among the dense trees here.

The best time to gather mushrooms is a few days after a fall downpour. The bronze leaves covering the pathways can make mushrooms hard to spot at first, but look again, and you are likely to see them all around. Soft, mossy verges become speckled with white, yellow, brown, black, and even purple toadstools. Peer up to spy wide, flat fungi climbing tree trunks, or gaze down at the ground to glimpse clusters of yellow mushrooms emerging from decomposing logs.

Not all of these fungi are edible, but there are many delectable specimens to be found. Around beech or birch trees, keep your eyes peeled for the yellow trumpeted top and wrinkled folds of the delicious chanterelle. And near oaks or pines, search for the stout stem and rounded cap of the prized porcini, also known as the cep or penny bun, which grows up to 10 in (25 cm) tall. Only pick something when you are 100 percent sure what it is—a foraging course or a guidebook should give you enough knowledge to give it a go.

Wood Wide Web

The mushrooms we recognize are just a small part of a much bigger picture—the mycelial network. Beneath our feet, huge underground webs of fungi connect plants and trees, sharing nutrients and passing messages along fine, wirelike filaments. This 450-million-year-old hidden social network has been christened the Wood Wide Web by scientists and is a crucial part of every forest ecosystem.

Right Inspecting mushrooms to make sure they're edible **Far right** A basket of wild mushrooms **Below** Walking through the forest on a foraging trip

Cross-Country Skiing

Also known as Nordic skiing, cross-country skiing is a world apart from its alpine cousin. There are no chairlifts to help with the uphills and fewer downhills where you can let gravity do the work—it all depends on you, a pair of poles, and two skinny, lightweight skis. All that extra effort brings with it a hugely rewarding mountain experience, though, with the chance to ski amid the serenity of beautiful backcountry.

Skiing through forest near Otepää, along the Tartu Maraton route

◁ OTEPÄÄ, ESTONIA

Learn to cross-country ski on a gentle trail through stunning pine forest in Estonia's winter capital.

Come winter, the Estonian town of Otepää is a place of Narnian landscapes, with thick pine forests, frozen lakes, and a picturesque carpet of pristine white snow. It's at this time of year that the town truly comes into its own—the country's official winter capital, Otepää is the largest alpine ski resort in the Baltics.

There are several downhill slopes here, but the best way to enjoy the winter wonderland is by gliding through it on a pair of cross-country skis. For proof of this fact, just look to the Estonian cross-country ski team, whose members train on the trails here, and to the thousands of entrants who flock to Otepää annually for the Tartu Maraton, a renowned cross-country skiing event.

The 39-mile (63 km) marathon route might be a little much for anyone new to the sport, but the well-established Pühajärve-Kääriku ski track is a great choice for beginners. This 6-mile (10 km) route has a gently rolling incline, allowing you to hone your technique on different gradients. It's straightforward to get started—the trail is free of charge, and you can arrange lessons through local outfitters.

Once you've got the hang of things, you can branch off onto one of the tougher, longer trails that link up with the track at Kääriku. And if you're really on a roll, you can keep going into the night—sections of the track are lit up in the evening, when you might find yourself accompanied by fox, deer, or wild rabbits scampering through the trees.

A cross-country skiing trail through the trees in Cerdagne-Capcir

△ CERDAGNE-CAPCIR, PYRENEES NATIONAL PARK, FRANCE

Discover the Catalan Pyrenees on a vast network of scenic cross-country ski trails.

Nestled at the border where France rubs shoulders with Spain and Andorra across the Pyrenees, Cerdagne-Capcir is an area of high-alpine lakes and Romanesque churches. Spread across this region are some of the best cross-country ski routes in France, an immense 280 miles (450 km) of trails dotted throughout the Neiges Catalanes ski area, from Sant-Pierres-dels-Forcats in Cerdagne up to Formiguères in Capcir.

There are six ski resorts here, but the best Nordic skiing is to be found in the mountainous areas away from these. Strap on your skis and start in the Domaine de la Llose, heading out in the crisp morning air on the breathtaking Le Dourmidou trail. This 8-mile (13 km) long track begins just east of La Llagonne and leads up a zigzagging path to a mirador with glorious views across to Mount Canigou. But there's so much to explore here that you don't need to limit yourself to a single trail—why not work your way around the beautiful high-plateau lake at the Domaine du Lac de l'Olive or try out the short stretch of nighttime track beside Lac de Matemale in the Domaine de la Forêt de la Matte. Whatever you do, make sure you save some time in your cross-country schedule for the trails at Cerdagne's Domaine du Rec del Moli—the tracks here are possibly the most scenic of all, winding through forest and over a frozen river up to a viewpoint overlooking the Mediterranean.

▷ SCHWANGAU, GERMANY

Glide through thick Bavarian forest with an iconic castle as your backdrop.

It's not often that you get to combine cross-country skiing with sightseeing—usually you're exploring quiet alpine corners, where there are minimal signs of civilization. But on the trails around the Bavarian village of Schwangau, you can enjoy glimpses of one of Germany's most famous monuments: Neuschwanstein Castle. There are 20 miles (32 km) of tracks in the area, crisscrossing the snowy forest and mountain-lined valley. For the best views, head to the beginner-friendly Neuschwanstein trail; it takes you directly below the castle's soaring turrets. Romantic at the best of times, the fortress looks especially enchanting when covered in snow—and even more so when viewed from the illuminated track at night.

Explore More

In addition to cross-country skiing routes, Schwangau also has a network of cleared winter hiking trails. There are 30 miles (50 km) of paths in total, punctuated by cozy mountain huts serving local snacks and warming mulled wine.

The Neuschwanstein trail, passing below the castle of the same name

White-beaked dolphins
leaping through the sea off
the Northumberland coast

Marine Wildlife Watching

Whether it's listening for the explosive exhale of a humpback whale or searching for seals by canoe, marine wildlife watching offers up plenty of opportunities for true adventure. But there's no need to get a toe wet if you don't want to—time it right, and you can spy a diverse range of playful aquatic creatures from the comfort of dry land.

◁ NORTHUMBERLAND, ENGLAND

In the warmer months, the playful white-beaked dolphin pays a visit to northeastern England's waters.

Take a summer stroll along the craggy Northumberland coastline and you shouldn't be surprised to see something leap clear of the water. Look a little closer and you might spot the silvery flash of a pale underbelly or the distinctive snout that gives the energetic white-beaked dolphin its name. Usually found in pods of five to 10 in UK waters, these dolphins are common in the cool currents of the North Atlantic. They're found year-round in the Hebrides and Devon's Lyme Bay, but they can often be tricky to spot. In the summer months, however, a number of white-beaked dolphins and their calves come very close to shore in Northumberland, where they work together to herd large shoals of fish and play in the wakes of boats. It's frequently possible to spot them with the naked eye, and observation can be carried out on land or via boat. Just be sure to keep a distance of at least 330 ft (100 m) if you come across the creatures while at sea.

Friendly Behavior

White-beaked dolphins are social animals, swimming not just with their own species but also with orca, humpback, minke, and fin whales. If alone, they'll forage for food by scooping up bottom-dwelling snacks from the sea floor, but they'll also often take part in group feedings, sharing shoals of fish with Atlantic white-sided dolphins and bottlenose dolphins, too.

▷ LAKE SAIMAA, FINLAND

Finland's ancient Saimaa lake district is the
only place on Earth where you can spot the
rare ringed seal.

At the end of the last Ice Age, the ringed seal found itself
in a bit of a predicament. A vast movement of ice had
separated it from other seals in the Baltic Sea, stranding
it on its own in an isolated environment. But these are
clever creatures—some scientists equate the animal's
intelligence levels to that of a domestic dog—and they
learned to adapt in their strange new home, eventually
evolving into a separate subspecies.

Today, there are approximately 400 seals living in the
Saimaa lake district, each one distinctly identifiable by its
unique fur pattern (just like a human's fingerprints). Over
time, they have developed characteristics that enable
them to thrive in the murky freshwaters of the lake, such
as large eyes to better deal with the dimness. And in
winter, when visibility under the ice is even poorer, they
find their way to hidden lairs and breathing holes using
their sensitive whiskers.

Spotting an animal that spends the majority of its life
underwater might sound tricky, but it can be done if you
know where and when to search. Toward the end of May,
the seals can often be observed, via boat, sprawled out
on top of the lakeshore rocks as they start to molt—when
the animals shed their fur, they also fast, so a lounge in
the sun helps them preserve energy. Sightings in winter
are less frequent, particularly in late February when the
mothers give birth to pups, nesting in lairs under the
snow drifts. But there's still a small chance you might
be lucky and find an adult near its breathing hole,
"sunbathing" on the ice.

A Helping Hand

Today, one of the greatest threats to the precious
Saimaa seal population is climate change, with
rising temperatures and a lack of snow making
breeding and birthing more difficult.
Thankfully, measures are in place to help the
seals survive, including a posse of human
volunteers who venture out onto the frozen lake
each winter to create artificial snow drifts. As
many as 90 percent of offspring are born each
year in these man-made nurseries.

Right A ringed seal swimming in one of Saimaa's lakes
Far right A ringed seal basking on a rock
Below The Saimaa lake district in Finland

Above The tail of a sperm whale flicking out of the water before a dive
Left A sperm whale diving beneath the surface, down to the depths of the ocean

◁ AZORES, PORTUGAL

Explore the deep-blue waters surrounding this Portuguese archipelago, home to a third of all whale species.

Iceland meets Hawaii in the Azores, a scattering of volcanic outcrops marooned in the mid-Atlantic partway between Portugal and North America. Fishing villages cling to the islands' rocky slopes, and the interiors are drenched in green or laced with the steam from thermal hot springs, their explosive origins still evident in crater lakes and lava caves. But it's offshore, in waters warmed by the Gulf Stream, where you'll find the true wonders of the Azores.

With 28 species of cetaceans recorded here, the island chain is one of the best places in the world to go whale watching—there are sightings on 99 percent of all trips. Head out on a boat from bustling Ponta Delgada harbor, on São Miguel, and you're almost guaranteed to see a sperm whale. They're easily recognized by their huge blocky heads and distinctive spout, which is sprayed forward rather than directly up; watching the graceful flick of a sperm whale's tail fluke before it disappears into the depths is one of Mother Nature's pinch-me moments. You're most likely to spy blue whales, the Earth's largest mammals, on boat trips leaving from Lajes do Pico, on the southern coast of Pico island, where the seabed is so deep that these ocean giants can come remarkably close to shore. Marine biologists are on hand with helpful spotting tips, so you can tell your Bryde's whales from your Blainville's beakeds; you just need to keep scanning the horizon, searching for that telltale puff of air.

Observing a young blue whale from a small boat in the Azores

Spotter's Guide

Sperm Whale

Sperm whales inhabit the Azores year-round and are named after the spermaceti (a waxy substance) that's found in their heads.

Blue Whale

Blue whales can grow up to 108 ft (33 m) long and, despite their name, often appear more gray than blue. They migrate through the Azores in spring.

Fin Whale

Nicknamed "greyhounds of the sea," fin whales can reach speeds of up to 29 mph (47 km/h). They inhabit the Azores year-round but are mainly seen in spring.

Humpback Whale

Recognizable by their knobbly heads, humpbacks pass through the Azores from March to May and in October, as they migrate between Cape Verde and Norway.

Pausing to admire the
otherworldly formations
in Optymistychna Cave

Caving

Caves are some of the least explored environments on Earth. Although the sport of caving—also known as potholing and spelunking—dates back as far as the 1840s, there are still corners that remain uncovered, even in the cave systems we know about. It's a different domain down there, a pristine hollow of tunnels, underground rivers, and eye-catching mineral formations. You can wander well-lit walkways or delve into the depths with a hard hat on and a headlight shining the way— either way, it's an adventure into another world.

-------------⋀-------------

Insider Tip

The temperature in Optymistychna remains a constant 50°F (10°C) all year round, so you'll need to wear warm layers. Tours include all the safety equipment you'll require— protective overall, boots, safety hat, and headlight.

▷ OPTYMISTYCHNA, UKRAINE

Admire the wondrous cave formations and jewel-like crystals that line the walls of this remote cavern.

The entrance doesn't look like much—a stone archway and a rusty metal door, set into wooded slopes on the outskirts of Korolivka village in the southwest corner of Ukraine. But behind the door and beneath the surface lies Optymistychna, the longest cave outside of the Americas, with 143 miles (230 km) of mapped passageways and who knows how much more still waiting to be found.

Discovered in 1966, Optimistic Cave, as it's known in English, was first opened to tourists in 2010. Seven routes, ranging from 2 miles (3 km) to 12 miles (18 km), wind through the cave complex—although you'd have to be a really committed caver if you wanted to tackle the longest of these, which requires spending more than 12 hours underground. The passages are small for the most part, around 10 ft (3 m) wide and 5 ft (1.5 m) tall, and in some cases you'll need to crawl through the tiniest of gaps.

But the squeeze will be worth it. Descending into the cave's chambers feels like a journey, if not to the center of the Earth then to the bottom of the ocean—huge crystals cluster along its walls, contorted into the craggy fingers of a glittering coral reef; yellow anthodites, long and needle-sharp, sprout from the rock face like sea urchins; and puffs of creamy moonmilk deposits hang from the ceiling in sponge-like clumps. It's a surreal landscape that feels like something straight out of science fiction.

▽ LA PIERRE SAINT-MARTIN, FRANCE

Big is definitely beautiful at this record-breaking karst cave system in southern France.

Everything about La Pierre Saint-Martin is huge. Part of a vast area of high karst that straddles the border between France and Spain, the cave system is one of the largest on Earth, with over a dozen entrances leading to 2,000 different cave chambers, several of which rank among the deepest in the world. The network was discovered in 1950, when French speleologist Georges Lépineux noticed a jackdaw flying out of a small black hole in the mountainside—the hole turned out to be the entranceway to a shaft so deep that it was nicknamed the Underground Everest.

Further explorations in the years since have revealed 270 miles (435 km) of winding passageways and immense caverns, including the jaw-dropping La Verna, the largest show cave in the world. It's so big, in fact, that in 2003 a team of French pilots flew a hot-air balloon around inside. Deeper into the system lie the Gallerie Aranzadi, along which a river originally flowed, and the almost equally vast Chevalier and Adélie caverns. Keep an eye out while you're exploring for some of the weird wildlife that ekes out an existence down here in the dark—blind beetles, fierce-looking centipedes, and other small creatures that look like mere specks compared to their vast surrounds.

Standing in the huge La Verna cavern at
La Pierre Saint-Martin

---

^

Insider Tip

Gaping Gill can be accessed by the public at "winch meets" run by a couple of local caving clubs. Bradford Pothole Club (*www.bpc-cave.org.uk*) runs its tour over the bank holiday in May; Craven Pothole Club (*www.cravenpotholeclub.org*) runs one for a week in August.

▷ YORKSHIRE DALES, ENGLAND

Descend into the darkness of some of Britain's most impressive caves.

Looking out over the Yorkshire Dales National Park, it's hard to believe that a vast network of underground caverns lies just below the surface of the rolling green moors. Actually, there are more than 2,500 known caves secreted throughout the limestone landscape here, drawing cavers from all over the UK and beyond. The most dramatic of these formations is Gaping Gill, the largest cave chamber in Britain (it's big enough to house St. Paul's Cathedral). Accessible just twice a year, via a small hole in the hills where a stream suddenly disappears into the earth, it can be entered only on a winch, accompanied by the sound of a thunderous waterfall echoing through the dark.

But Gaping Gill isn't the only superlative in these parts; the Dales are also home to Ease Gill, part of the Three Counties System—at around 55 miles (89 km) long, it's the most extensive cave system in Britain. Here, you can scramble around curiously named caverns such as Cow Dubs and Wretched Rabbit and move between three different counties entirely underground.

Surfing

Surfing is one of the most nature-intensive experiences on Earth. Whether
you're a seasoned pro or just starting out, riding waves lets you harness
the energy of the ocean in its purest form, immersing you in its power
and roar. Surfing is a buzz, of course, but being on your board in water
also calms the mind and helps you escape the everyday—positive
effects scientists now refer to as "blue health."

▷ CORNWALL, ENGLAND

Surf Cornwall's wild and rugged northern coastline,
at the beating heart of the British wave-riding scene.

There are plenty of places to surf in the UK, but there is
nowhere quite like northern Cornwall. The magic comes
not just from the quality and consistency of the waves here,
fueled by deep low-pressure systems in the Atlantic, but
from the spectacular backdrop that frames each surf
session. The crumbling cliffs and green rolling hills, the
sandy beaches and sheltered coves (once beloved by
smugglers), and the vast head-clearing skies.

Don't head there in summer, when it's packed with
vacationers and the waves are often flat; instead, come
in the off season. Who cares about blue skies when the
water holds a decent 55°F (13°C) until November? And if
you have the right cold-water gear, you can surf all year
round, except when the big storms hit. Newquay is the
county's unofficial wave-riding capital, but you'll find
surf spots for all levels along the entire length of this
enchanting stretch of coast.

Surfers Against Sewage

In 1990, fed up with paddling through raw
sewage to catch waves, a group of surfers from
St. Agnes in Cornwall set up a charity to
improve coastal water quality. Today, Surfers
Against Sewage (*www.sas.org.uk*) is a hugely
successful environmental charity and the UK
now has some of the cleanest beaches in Europe.

" *The dominant winds blow away from shore, enabling long rides on clean, photogenic peaks that look ripped from the pages of a magazine.* "

Left Riding the waves in
Portrush, County Antrim
Below The golden sands of
the beach at Portrush

▽ KLITMØLLER, DENMARK

In Klitmøller, Denmark has its own iteration of
Hawaii—albeit with considerably colder water
and infamous winter storms.

A small working fishing village, Klitmøller is known to
locals as "Cold Hawaii" on account of its reputation as
northern Europe's most hardy surf spot. It certainly lives
up to the first part of its nickname: the coast here is
windswept and weather-battered, with a heavy Atlantic
swell coming from Iceland and the Faroe Islands. But the
wildness of the conditions means that rideable waves
arrive almost every day, and a close-knit community of
adventurous surfers has been steadily growing here since
the early 1990s. The atmosphere on the water is friendly,
with the unusual sight of stand-up paddleboarders,
windsurfers, and regular surfers all mixing amicably
together—bonded by the shared delight at having
discovered one of Denmark's most unexpected treasures.

◁ PORTRUSH, NORTHERN IRELAND

This picturesque town in County Antrim, at the
heart of the Causeway Coast, is a buzzing hub of
Northern Irish surfing.

For most surfers in Britain, the prevailing winds are
nothing but a curse to their wave-riding; they're either
onshore (toward the land), causing waves to topple
too early, or cross shore (parallel to the land), which
ruins their shape. But in Portrush, on the north coast
of County Antrim, the dominant winds blow away from
shore, enabling long rides on clean, photogenic peaks
that look ripped from the pages of a magazine.

The first surf club was established in Portrush in
the late 1960s, and the pretty seaside resort has been
a pioneer of the Northern Irish surf scene ever since—
it's the hometown of six-times all-Ireland champion
Andrew Hill, who nowadays runs a surf shop here. The
main surfing spots are West Strand and East Strand,
set on either side of a 1-mile (2 km) long peninsula,
with golden sand and sweeping views of the dramatic
Causeway headlands. Each strip of coast offers a
different surfing experience, with West Strand known
for the consistency of its waves and East Strand famed
for its powerful winter swell. Both draw surfers from
around the world, but you don't have to be an expert
to ride the waves here—the friendly vibe and deeply
ingrained local surfing culture mean that it's a highly
welcoming place for beginners, too.

Warming up before a surf lesson in Klitmøller,
otherwise known as "Cold Hawaii"

▷ COMPORTA, PORTUGAL

Comporta is one of Portugal's lesser-known surf spots, offering a relaxed wave-riding experience surrounded by untamed nature.

Portugal is a world-class surf destination with well-known spots dotted along its Atlantic coastline, from the big wave mecca of Nazare to the barrels of Supertubos, on the edge of Peniche. But if you're looking to surf somewhere with a wild and remote feel, and with a lineup that doesn't involve tricky starts or jostling with experts, seek out the stretch of beach at Comporta.

Just over an hour's drive south from Lisbon, Comporta lies at the foot of the Troia peninsula between the Sado Estuary and Alentejo, the country's rural center. The region is made up of seven villages, where strict local building diktats have guarded against any unsightly developments. Instead of sprawling resorts, you'll see thatched cabanas, converted fishing huts, and low-rise driftwood architecture aplenty. The landscape here is lush—irrigation canals feed verdant rice paddy fields, fruit and vegetable plants grow in abundance, and unspoiled dunes tumble into forests dense with pine and cork oak trees.

This laid-back, natural feel extends to the wave-riding. Comporta is a beach break, meaning the waves break over sand rather than a reef, so there's a soft landing if you fall off your board. And although the Atlantic is known for being on the cool side, the ocean and air temperatures in summer and early fall are warm enough that there's no need to wear a full wet suit (making movement a lot freer).

From the water, you're greeted by views of a seemingly endless strip of fine white sand, backed by a tangle of green vegetation rolling over the dunes. The extensive run of beach here is a popular getaway for well-heeled residents of Lisbon in July and August, but even at peak times, it never feels packed. You can just focus on you, your board, and the shifting of the sea, perhaps even glimpsing one of the bottlenose dolphins that live around the Sado Estuary.

Comporta translates as "floodgate," which makes sense as the place feels in many ways like a last restraint against the wave of modernity that's swept across countless other pretty coastlines in Portugal. Riding the waves here, as the sun melts into the ocean and the sky is streaked a neon pink, can almost feel like you're surfing in a forgotten world.

Insider Tip

Surf in Comporta *(www. surfincomporta.com)* hosts several surf camps throughout the year. If you're a new or inexperienced surfer, and especially if you're a solo traveler, these are a great way to meet people while having fun safely in the waves.

Above Coasting atop
the crest of a wave at
Comporta
Far left A scattering
of sunbathers along the
beach at Comporta
Left Sitting on a
surfboard, waiting
to catch a wave

Flora Spotting

A feast for the senses, flora spotting uncovers the plant kingdom's most beautiful sights and smells, whether it's a vista of bright wildflowers or a sweet-scented blossom. Each country and every season presents a fresh face, opening up new landscapes of flora, each distinctive and bewitching in their own way.

A meadow filled with bright yellow globeflowers, overlooked by the peak of the Jungfrau

◁ WENGEN, SWITZERLAND

The mountain meadows of Wengen, found high in the Swiss Alps, come alive with an abundance of colorful wildflowers every summer.

There's much to recommend the Swiss mountain village of Wengen. Cozy wooden chalets hang prettily on the lush green mountainsides; the fresh smell of pine lingers in the clean, clear air; and the clouds are so close it feels like you could reach up and touch them. Watching over the whole scene are the sheer, snow-frosted peaks of the Eiger and Jungfrau.

This tranquil spot becomes even more beautiful in June and July, when a riot of wildflowers erupts in the Alpine meadows surrounding the village. Hiking through the hills, you might spot the golden, shoelike flowers of the lady's slipper orchid and the spherical yellow petals of the globeflower, as well as masses of trumpet-shaped, deep-blue gentians. As you wander, the sweet, citrusy smell of primrose wafts by on the breeze, while the air buzzes with the sound of busy bumblebees.

Clusters of *Orchis italica*
strewn colorfully across
the Cretan landscape

▷ CRETE, GREECE

Walk among the wondrous wildflowers of Crete,
where orchids resembling both human figures and
honey bees carpet the floors of plunging canyons.

No flower evokes a sense of exotic beauty and mystery
like the orchid, variously prized since ancient times as a
symbol of power and elegance, fertility and death. Orchids
include some of the rarest flowers on earth but make up
a vast family; there are four times as many species of
orchids as there are mammals, with around 70 found on
the gorgeous island of Crete.

Tucked away in Crete's mountainous interior is the Rouva
Gorge, where rivers burble through groves of olive and
carob, and the ruins of monks' hermitages crumble
elegantly into the stony hillsides. Come here in spring
and you might spot the blotchy monochrome patterns of
Ariadne's Ophrys, named for a mythical Cretan princess,
or smell the intoxicating honeylike scent of Robert's giant
orchid. West of Rouva lie the fragrant pine woodlands of
Kourtaliotis—visit these at the same time of year, and
you'll be rewarded with the magnificent sight of the
heroic butterfly orchid in full bloom, its petals a
spellbinding riot of pink and white.

Spring also brings the chance to glimpse two of Crete's
most unusual orchids. In the meadows of Rethymno, you'll
spy the bee orchid—this amazing plant has evolved to
mimic its furry, gold-and-black lookalike. Meanwhile, the
island's phrygana scrublands play host to *Orchis italica*,
known as the naked-man orchid for the humanlike shape
of its spiky flowers. As you wander past each unique bloom,
it's easy to see why so many before you have been
entranced by these enchanting flowers.

Preserving Crete's Orchids

Crete is justifiably popular as a vacation
destination, but the island's rampant
development—driven by investors
building vacation homes on meadows and
woodland—has placed its fragile orchids under
threat. Grazing flocks of goats and sheep, and
pesticides that kill the bees that pollinate the
orchids, are further causes for concern.
Efforts are underway by conservation groups
like Flowers of Crete *(www.flowersofcrete.info)*
to relocate orchids from property
development sites and to establish reserves
where the threatened species can flourish.

Robert's Giant Orchid

This huge orchid grows up to
3 ft (1 m) in height, and has big
pink-and-white flowers.

Bee Orchid

The bee orchid not only looks
like its namesake but shares its
hairy texture, too.

Ariadne's Ophrys

Perhaps Crete's most lovely orchid,
with inkblotlike patterns of white
and dark purple on large flowers.

Orchis Italica

The naked-man orchid can grow
up to 20 in (50 cm) tall and is
usually pink but occasionally white.

Far left Bluebell stems laden with delicate flowers
Left A squirrel standing amid the bluebells
Below A carpet of bluebells in Ashenbank Wood

Above Hiking among the giant evergreens of the Caucasus Nature Reserve

◁ CAUCASUS NATURE RESERVE, RUSSIA

Deep in Russia's Western Caucasus, crane your neck skyward and admire the tallest trees in Europe.

When it comes to nature, Russia doesn't do things by halves. This vast country—the largest in the world—is home to Europe's biggest lake, its highest mountain, and its tallest trees. The latter is the mighty Nordmann fir, which looms above the Caucasus Nature Reserve, a vast swathe of oversized Christmas trees that stretches from the shores of the Black Sea to the slopes of the soaring Caucasus range. Native to the mountains of Turkey, Georgia, and western Russia, the firs are a relic—when you walk among these giants, you're surrounded by the descendants of vast forests dating from the last Ice Age, around 100,000 years ago.

These soaring evergreens have been known to reach the gargantuan heights of 280 ft (85 m)—almost as tall as London's Big Ben—and their trunks alone can grow to 6 ft (2 m) in diameter. As the boughs of these firs spread out high above the forest floor and the sun filters down in bright beams, the forest can feel like a natural cathedral made of wood, leaf, and light. Here, a fresh, somewhat citrusy smell drifts through the still air, and there's a peaceful, almost profound, sense of quiet beneath the insulating canopy of dark-green needles.

---⋀---

Explore More

Also found within the Caucasus Nature Reserve is the magical Khosta Grove. This subtropical forest, located near the coast, contains more than 400 species of plants. An undoubted highlight are the ancient yew trees that have been twisting and contorting themselves into knots here for 2,000 years.

◁ ASHENBANK WOOD, ENGLAND

England's ancient woodlands erupt each spring in a violet-hued riot of magic and mystery.

Is there a sight more English or more lovely than bluebells blanketing the floor of a springtime wood? Like the defiance of snowdrops against a frosty morning or the gathering inferno of fall leaves, the emergence of these flowers marks the changing of the seasons. To walk among bluebells is to step into the past—they grow only in ancient woodlands, such as the magical Ashenbank Wood in Kent. These violet-blue blooms are also wreathed in mythology and folklore. In fact, it's often said that they are the enchanted domain of fairies, who use the flowers' beauty to bewitch humans and trap them there forever—a fate that, once you've spent some time in this otherworldly woodland, doesn't sound so bad.

Tobogganing

Skidding down a snowy, icy, or artificial slope on a sleigh or toboggan (a sleigh without the runners) provides a burst of excitement that whisks you straight back to your childhood. This is one of the easiest, least expensive, and most enjoyable winter sports, regardless of your age. At its simplest, all you need is something smooth and flat to sit on and a snow-covered hill to slide down. But there are also scores of resorts, centers, and specially designed runs across Europe that elevate tobogganing to the next level.

Sliding down the winding, tree-lined Korketrekkeren toboggan run

◁ KORKETREKKEREN, OSLO, NORWAY

Spiral down the "Corkscrew" on the forested northern fringe of the Norwegian capital.

There aren't many toboggan tracks as conveniently located as the Korketrekkeren ("Corkscrew" in Norwegian). Hop on the Metro in downtown Oslo, and in half an hour or so you'll reach Frognerseteren, a tobogganing center for almost 150 years. This is the starting point for the 1-mile (2 km) Korketrekkeren, a completely free track packed with spiraling twists and coiling turns—a reminder of its original incarnation as a luge and bobsleigh run. Bring your own sledge or rent one from the center to slide down the run's winding, pine-fringed slope to the neighborhood of Midtstuen. The ride takes 8–10 minutes—roughly half the time the same journey takes on the Metro. When you reach the end of the run (just a few steps away from Midtstuen station), you simply pick up your sleigh, jump back on the train to Frognerseteren, and do it all over again.

Zooming along the Cosmojet, surrounded by snowy mountains

△ COSMOJET, VAL THORENS, FRANCE

Slide down one of Europe's longest toboggan runs at a high-altitude resort in the French Alps.

While some toboggan runs are over in a flash, the Cosmojet provides plenty of time to savor the experience. It takes around 45 minutes for beginners to complete this popular 4-mile (6 km) route at the resort of Val Thorens, though the most accomplished tobogganers can finish it in less than a quarter of that time with an average speed of around 22 mph (36 km/h). Starting off from the base of the Péclet glacier, which is 9,843 ft (3,000 m) above sea level, the piste has plenty of banked turns, bends, zigzags, and tunnels—not to mention sweeping views of the surrounding snow-packed mountains—to keep things interesting. Once you've got the hang of things, try out the atmospheric nighttime runs, when helmet torches help light up the route.

Insider Tip

Val Thorens is the highest winter sports resort in Europe and, as a result, has a longer season than most of its counterparts. Some years you can toboggan here from the start of December to as late as mid-May.

"Snow tubing" down the runs
at the Swiss resort of Leysin

▷ LEYSIN, SWITZERLAND

Try your hand at "snow tubing" at a Swiss winter sports resort. The runs are reminiscent of bobsled courses and were designed by an Olympic medalist.

The competitive sport of sledding first originated in the Swiss Alps in the 1880s, and Switzerland has a proud tradition of producing world-class competitors, particularly in the bobsled. So it's no surprise that the region is today home to some of the longest, fastest, and most creative sledding and tobogganing runs in the world. Several of the best are found at the Tobogganing Park, a winter sports center that offers an accessible modern twist on this age-old activity from December to March.

Located in the attractive resort town of Leysin, which sits at the base of the Tour d'Aï mountain, the park specializes in "snow tubing." This involves sitting in the middle of a large inflatable rubber ring, strapping on a helmet, and gliding down one of a number of quicksilver runs. The serpentine courses—designed by a team supported by former bobsled world champion and Olympic medalist Silvio Giobellina—have banked sides to keep you on track and feature a dizzying array of bends, twists, and corners. Some feature tunnels, 360-degree turns, and loop-the-loops to further discombobulate you. The surrounding scenery—think classic Alpine peaks, thick evergreen forests, and even clusters of igloos built by the park's staff—is spectacular, but you'll be too caught up in the moment to pay much attention to it.

In total, the Toboggan Park has more than 1.7 miles (2.8 km) of runs, so there's plenty to keep even the most ardent of snow tubers busy. You can try them out on your own or, on some of the runs, slide down one by one as part of a small group. There are a couple of shorter, simpler tracks for children aged four and above at the on-site "mini park," as well as numerous faster and more complicated ones designed for older children and adults. On some of the latter, you can reach a top speed of up to 37 mph (60 km/h). All of the runs come to the same exhilarating conclusion—a jump that launches you up into the air for a few breathless moments before depositing you and your inflatable ring safely onto a giant airbag.

The First Toboggan Race

The first official toboggan race took place in Davos, Switzerland, in 1883. Run along a 2.5-mile (4 km) course between the villages of St. Wolfgang and Klosters, it featured competitors from around the world. The joint winners were Swiss postman Peter Minsch and Australian student George Robertson, who finished together in a dead heat. This race is considered the forerunner of the modern winter sport that today encompasses three Olympic events—bobsled, skeleton and luge.

Flying down one of the mountain bike trails in magical Davagh Forest

Mountain Biking

Tearing down a precipitous dirt track, navigating tangled roots on a testing forest trail, or cresting a hill on a leisurely cross-country route—mountain biking offers an incredible range of experiences. Bike parks—imagine ski resorts but designed for mountain bikes—and dedicated cross-country trails have sprung up across the continent, so there are more options than ever before, whatever your interests or level of ability.

▷ DAVAGH FOREST, NORTHERN IRELAND

Develop your skills on one of the trails looping through this rugged, mountainous forest.

Nestled in the heart of the Sperrins Mountains—once the stomping ground of bandits and outlaws—the misty, cloistered Davagh Forest provides an excellent training ground for eager mountain bikers. Warm up at the skills area, whose practice sections provide a great place to perfect your technique, and then get your blood properly flowing on one of the forest's three loops, each a different difficulty level. The Green trail offers mellow slaloms through moss-covered trees that are perfect for beginners, while the Blue trail—with its adrenaline-pumping flow sections of jumps and berms (corners with banked outer edges) that snake down steep hillsides—will challenge your abilities. Once you've refined your technique, and you're feeling courageous enough, take the Red trail over Eagles' Rock and Boundary Rock. With its white-knuckle single-track, tight berms and gut-clenching rock drops, this route will test your limits.

▽ HAFJELL BIKE PARK, NORWAY

This hilltop bike park has gained a reputation
for the sheer variety of its trails.

Lillehammer might have a world-class reputation for
winter sports, but in the summer, mountain biking draws
the crowds. Found just out of town, Hafjell Bike Park
offers terrain for every type of rider, plus some of
Europe's best lift-accessed mountain biking.

The park's Mosetertoppen area, with its long pump
track of small rollers and quick turns, is a great place for
beginners to learn the ropes. From there, you can hone
your skills on a range of different trails. Want to give free-
riding (doing tricks and stunts as you zoom downhill) a
go? Try Parkløypa. This route—full of smooth, banked
turns and a variety of jumps, both big and small—will leave
your stomach in your chest. Or test your balance on Old
School, a greatest-hits trail from the early days of mountain
biking, where you can pick your way through the forest,
navigating tight turns, side slopes, and conifer roots.
From here, you can take the chairlift to the gnarlier terrain
up high or jump on the gondola—which has easy access
ideal for adaptive riders—back to the Mosetertoppen area.

If you're a mountain biking master, however, there's no
better trail to test yourself on than the World Cup Downhill
track, which has rattled the bones of the world's best riders.
Set off from the starting gate straight into a series of jumps,
followed by a speedy, hair-raising descent through a rock
garden. The pros do this 1-mile (1.6 km) screamer in three-
and-a-half minutes—how close can you get?

A mountain biker leaping over a jump on
one of Hafjell Bike Park's many routes

---^---

Explore More

Based on a 3,944 ft (1,202 m)
hill just north of Šumava
National Park, Bike Park
Spicak has several adrenaline-
charged downhill mountain-
biking trails tailored to
everyone from novices to
pros, as well as a jump center
and skills area. Once you've
got the hang of things, check
out its longest run—the 1.4-
mile (2.3 km) Black Friday—
which features plenty of
jumps and berms.

▷ ŠUMAVA, CZECH REPUBLIC

Forget the downhill scene—this mountainous region
in south Bohemia is laced with cross-country routes.

Extending across the German border into Bavaria,
Šumava is a low mountain range made up of ancient
forests, glacial lakes, and peat bogs. This undulating
region is best explored by mountain bike, thanks to the
countless tarmac, gravel, and dirt trails that crisscross
the landscape. While some of these involve steep ascents
and require a great deal of stamina, other trails are flat
and easygoing. As a leisurely introduction, enjoy a
peaceful cruise along the network of smooth paths in
Šumava National Park, whose dense woodlands are part
of a UNESCO Biosphere Reserve. If you're hankering after
a greater physical test, try cycling one of the routes that
take in the vast, triangular Black Lake—overlooked by
towering peaks, it is the largest and deepest body of
water in the Czech Republic.

Right Trail through Šumava's forest
Far right Cycling along another of the park's paths
Below Resting by the expansive Black Lake

Speeding down a
track at Geisskopf
Bike Park

◁ GEISSKOPF BIKE PARK, GERMANY

In the heart of the Bavarian Forest, challenge yourself
on inventive trails at this pioneering mountain-
biking center.

Stretching for around 62 miles (100 km) along the border
with the Czech Republic, Germany's Bavarian Forest is
renowned for its peaceful woodlands, majestic mountains,
and extensive hiking trails. It's also home to a wealth of
wildlife, including lynx, otters, capercaillies, Ural owls,
and over 2,000 species of fungi. But among mountain
bikers across Europe, the area has a rather different
claim to fame—it's the site of the oldest bike park on
the continent, Geisskopf.

The park is based on the 3,599 ft (1,097 m) high
Geisskopf mountain, which rises above the municipality of
Bischofsmais. A chairlift transports riders and their bikes
up to the summit, from where there are views of the peaks,
hills, and forests for which the region is famous. But these
impressive vistas are only a momentary distraction from
the multitude of trails that slither down the mountain
slopes. Combining steep descents, slaloms, jumps, several
different surfaces (including dirt trails, stony paths, and
wooden tracks) and a variety of other obstacles, they offer
riders a heady mix of thrills and, occasionally, spills.

In total, there are 15 trails at Geisskopf ranging in length
from 984 ft to 1.9 miles (300 m to 3 km). If you're a beginner,
there are several short, straightforward routes (such as
Dual Slalom and X Ride) where you can familiarize yourself
with your bike, develop your skills, and build up your confidence. A wide range of lessons and courses, lasting from
a few hours to several days, are also available if needed.
Meanwhile, more experienced riders can try their hand
at some of the more challenging trails. These include

The Origins of Geisskopf

Founded in 1999, Geisskopf is Europe's oldest
bike park. The man behind it is former professional cyclist Diddie Schneider, now an award-
winning and highly influential trail designer.
Schneider, who has designed bike parks around
the world, believes enjoyment and accessibility
are crucial elements. "A good bike park is not
defined by difficulties and risks but by diversity
and the biking experience. And that must be
available for [riders of] all skill levels," he says.

the deceptively named Downhill and the more ominous-
sounding Evil Eye 2.0, both of which are inventive, technically demanding rides. Some of the trails are suitable
for electric mountain bikes, most notably Uphill Flow, which,
in a novel twist, involves a long, scenic ascent. There are
also areas of the complex where pros can show off their
jumps, bar spins, back flips, tail whips, and other gravity-
defying tricks.

But Geisskopf is probably best known for the award-
winning 1.6-mile (2.5 km) Flow Country Trail. On this
all-weather, family-friendly route, pedaling is kept to
a minimum, so riders can fully immerse themselves in
the descent. The aim of the designers was to create a
trail that feels like riding a roller coaster and generates
a sense of pure euphoria. To say that they've met their
objectives is an understatement, as anyone who sails
along the smooth, hard surfaces, skims across the jumps,
and swoops around the wide bends of the Flow Country
Trail can testify.

Mountaineering

Tackling big peaks is challenging. There's the physical test of the climb, usually at altitude, and the technical nature of it—you'll often have to use ice axes, crampons, and climbing gear. But it also gives a sense of perspective. On a mountain, the mind, freed from the distractions of the modern world, settles into a wonderfully uncomplicated routine: climb, rest, repeat. And, at the summit, all the hardship washes away— after all, nothing compares to standing on the rooftops of the world.

◁ MOUNT ELBRUS, RUSSIA

This mighty double-coned volcano offers would-be mountaineers the chance to cut their teeth.

When people think of mountaineering in Europe, they invariably conjure up the Alps. But those wanting to tackle the continent's highest summit need to head 1,740 miles (2,800 km) further east to Russia's Caucasus Mountains— here, the twin cones of Mount Elbrus rise 18,510 ft (5,642 m) into the sky.

Despite its imposing stature, Elbrus can be scaled by more than just hard-core mountaineers: in fact, there's no need to have previous mountaineering experience, as the route involves hardly any technical climbing. Providing you're fit and open to foregoing comforts for a few days, reaching the "rooftop of Europe" is indeed attainable. If you're an experienced mountaineer, you may consider a solo attempt, but most would-be summiteers enlist the services of a guiding company, who can offer crash courses in basic mountaineering skills en route. ▶

Climbing through snow toward the summit of Mount Elbrus, as the rising sun illuminates the surrounding peaks

Acute Mountain Sickness

Altitude sickness, also known as Acute Mountain Sickness (AMS), occurs at altitude, when the body cannot take in enough oxygen. Symptoms usually appear above 8,200 ft (2,500 m)—if lucky, a climber might get away with some shortness of breath and mild headaches, but more severe symptoms include loss of appetite, difficulty sleeping, vomiting and, in the worst cases, death. To prevent AMS, mountaineers take multiple acclimatization hikes before the summit day and drink lots of fluids throughout the climb.

This doesn't mean that the summit is easily won, however. Not only will you have to be comfortable with carrying a 26 lb (12 kg) pack, walking for more than 12 hours and ascending up to 4,900 ft (1,500 m) every day, you'll also have to be lucky with the weather, which is notoriously changeable. It's quite normal to be sweating beneath clear skies and hot summer sun one minute, only to be pulling on protective clothing as a blizzard sets in moments later.

After last-minute gear checks and acclimatization hikes (the latter essential to prevent Acute Mountain Sickness), you'll set off from the alpine village of Terskol, heading for the ski station at Azau, on the lower slopes of Mount Elbrus. From here, the multiday ascent begins in earnest with a long hike up to the scattering of rudimentary huts at around 12,800 ft (3,900 m), used by most climbing teams as a base camp.

After arriving at the huts, there are several days of hikes to help you acclimatize and hone your mountaineering skills before the final summit push. The evenings are typically spent milling around camp chatting to fellow climbers and soaking up the golden sunsets. After a tough day on the slopes, there are few things more rewarding than watching the evening alpenglow linger on a frozen peak before the hostile chill of night sends you running to your sleeping bag.

Summit day is tough, so don't underestimate it. You'll rise in the dead of night, moving up the snow-covered lower slopes with nothing but a head torch for light. As the sun appears, your extremities will warm, but the daylight also reveals the magnitude of the challenge still ahead. The route is a steady march through deep snow, skirting up around the volcanic cone of the East Summit and onto the Saddle, a broad flat col that bisects the two peaks. Here, you'll rest for a final time, before tackling the steeper—and higher—West Summit, which includes around 1,600 ft (500 m) of fixed-rope climbing.

When you finally reach the West Summit of Elbrus, after almost 12 hours of footslogging, you'll likely be dehydrated, exhausted, and gasping for air. But that will all be forgotten within moments as you bask in the glory of reaching the crown of Europe. As with most high-altitude summits, celebrations on the top of Mount Elbrus are often short-lived—there's still a four-hour descent back to the base camp huts after all—but always spectacular. From the top of the peak on a clear day, waves of jagged Caucasus peaks greet the eye and steal what remaining breath you may have left.

MONT BLANC, FRANCE

The "White Mountain" is widely considered the birthplace of modern mountaineering.

In 1786, two local mountaineers—Jacques Balmat and Dr. Michel Gabriel Paccard—were the first people to reach the 15,774 ft (4,808 m) summit of Mont Blanc, the Alp's highest mountain. This astounding achievement was considered to be the first instance of modern mountaineering, and since then, Mont Blanc's dizzying peak has been regarded as a rite of passage for anyone into Alpinism (as mountaineering is known in France). Today, several routes scale Mont Blanc, with the two- to three-day Goûter Route the busiest and most popular. This north-face climb isn't overly technical, so if you're fairly fit, have some basic mountaineering skills, and, of course, a guide with you, this exhilarating ascent is within reach.

Top left Ascending the snowy slopes of Mont Blanc, surrounded by floating clouds

GRAN PARADISO, ITALY

Mountaineering in Italy's Graian Alps is all about stunning scenery and local wildlife.

Gran Paradiso (13,323 ft/4,061 m) is the highest point in the national park of the same name. Scaling this peak is heavy on legwork (unlike other spots in the Alps, there aren't lifts to get you partway up), but the wild scenery more than makes up for it. Both of the two main trails to the summit snake through larch forests and Alpine meadows up to rougher, rockier terrain. On the way, you might spot long-horned Alpine ibex— the park's emblem—as well as chamois, mountain hare, and golden eagles. Your rope and crampon skills will be put to the test tackling the glacial section on the final summit ridge—but this painstaking early morning ascent is rewarded when the snowy Alps are lit up one by one by the rising sun.

Bottom left Reaching the high, rocky summit of Gran Paradiso, the highest peak in Italy's Graian Alps

KEBNEKAISE, SWEDEN

Climb through pristine Lapland wilderness to summit Sweden's highest peak.

Deep in the Arctic Circle, this 6,900 ft (2,106 m) high peak has two routes from Kebnekaise Mountain Station to its icy summit: east (østra) and west (västra). You can go it alone on the western route, but the steeper and more challenging eastern trail requires a guide as it crosses a snowy glacier and takes in a vertiginous section of via ferrata. Either route is a 12-hour test of endurance through the untouched Arctic wilds— high winds can whip up at any time and the shifting rocks beneath your feet can make the going tricky—so your climb is best undertaken under the summer midnight sun. The going is tough, but on the way, you can drink in views of snow-clad peaks that stretch before you in all directions.

Top right Hiking through open meadowland on the way to scale Kebnekaise

MULHACEN, SPAIN

The "Roof of Spain" lures experienced mountaineers to its summit during winter.

Part of the staggering Sierra Nevada mountain range in southern Spain, Mulhacen soars 11,414 ft (3,479 m) . During summer, the trails winding up the south face make for a pretty straightforward hike; but come the deep snow of winter, it's another story. Then, crampons and an ice ax are compulsory companions, and excellent navigating skills are a must—once you pass the snow line, the paths will be completely covered. The air, cool and thin year-round this high up, has a particularly sharp bite to it, too. But it all adds to the exhilaration of reaching mainland Spain's highest point; from the summit, views can stretch as far as the Mediterranean and coast of Morocco.

Bottom right Mountaineers walking up the lower slopes of Mulhacen, the highest summit in mainland Spain

Windsurfing

Riding on a sailboard with the wind at your back, carving a wake through the ocean blue—windsurfing is one of the most exhilarating ways to explore the waves. A cross between surfing and sailing, the sport requires you to balance on a board while holding onto a sail, simultaneously riding the waves and being carried by the winds. First-timers should make for flatter water with an experienced guide, who can provide all the necessary equipment, while experts can test themselves with windier conditions and bigger waves.

▷ SOTAVENTO BEACH, FUERTEVENTURA, CANARY ISLANDS

Test your windsurfing mettle on huge, World Championship–level waves in the Canary Islands.

Sotavento Beach stretches for a whopping 6 miles (9 km) down the east coast of Fuerteventura. It's uniquely beautiful—think golden sweeps of sand lapped by vivid turquoise waters, beneath which the silvery flash of a porgy or the electric-blue fin of a canary damselfish might catch your eye. But visitors don't come here for the stunning scenery: instead, it's Sotavento's reputation as a windsurfing mecca that draws the crowds—this is, after all, the long-standing home of the Windsurfing and Kiteboarding World Cup.

All levels of expertise are welcome. Here, calm and flat stretches are perfect for beginners taking to a sailboard for the first time, while strong trade winds help experienced riders rival the pros and hit speeds of more than 50 mph (80km/h). If you're a freestyle windsurfer, you'll want to head to the Sotavento Lagoon, which appears at low tide just off the central area of the beach; the relatively flat water here is ideal for performing tricks, spinning and rotating your sail around you as you dance on your board.

Insider Tip

While a regular swimming costume can be used as windsurfing attire, most windsurfers don a rash vest to guard against chafing and protect from the sun. Rubber or neoprene water shoes can also be a good idea for beginners, offering extra grip.

If it's big waves you're after, head north of the lagoon, where high winds ensure a particularly good line in left-handers (waves that break to the left-hand side). The blustery conditions at this end of the beach are caused by the so-called "Sotavento wind funnel," whereby the northeasterly wind accelerates between the peaks of two mountains. As you skid over the powerful waves, the wind whipping your face and the surf spraying all around, the area's name—Costa Calma ("calm coast")—could leave you scratching your head.

Windsurfing over
Sotavento's glimmering
turquoise waters

▷ PORTO POLLO, SARDINIA, ITALY

A quiet crest of sand on Sardinia's pristine coastline promises gorgeous Mediterranean views and ideal weather for novice and expert windsurfers alike.

The pleasingly named Porto Pollo—Chicken Harbor—is a crescent bay on Sardinia's northern coast, where high winds and varied waves combine to make perfect conditions for windsurfers. For some three decades, Porto Pollo's secret had been jealously guarded by local surfers, drawn in by the mistral: the stiff, chilly northwesterly wind that sweeps the Mediterranean from southern France. Then, in 1980, windsurfing legend and pioneer Robby Naish paid a visit and was enchanted by the bay's beauty and its possibilities for sailing both on "meter-high chops and on water as flat as a salt lake." He had found, as he put it, the perfect natural gym for windsurfers, and his endorsement led to Porto Pollo's establishment as a windsurfing hot spot.

The varied conditions mean Porto Pollo is a friendly spot for windsurfers of all ability levels. Different times of day are better for different experience levels: the mornings see flat water conditions, ideal for beginners, while afternoons—once the wind has risen and the waves start to roll in—are best for more seasoned windsurfers. For those taking to the water for the first time, a cluster of wooden shacks at the northern end of the beach offer equipment and lessons.

Whether you're a windsurfing pro or are just starting out, one thing is for certain—the views will be remarkable. From the water, you'll have unobstructed vistas over the half-moon bay, where a thin isthmus of ivory sand connects the Sardinian mainland to the lonely Isola dei Gabbiani; this island's wind-whipped shores, tufted with wild grasses and gorse, make for an atmospheric sight as they rise out of the cobalt waters. The scent of lavender and juniper carries on the wind from the dunes that stretch inland from the beach, while in the distance, you can make out the craggy expanse of the uninhabited Isola Spargi. As you skim across the ocean, stunning scenery all around, it's difficult to imagine a better spot for windsurfing.

Left Skimming across Porto Pollo's golden seas at sunset
Below Gliding over blue waters, surrounded by beautiful coastline

▽ DINGLE PENINSULA, IRELAND

This verdant sliver of green at the westernmost tip of Europe is a great place to learn the ropes.

Windsurfers of all stripes are drawn to this emerald finger of Atlantic coastline—but it's the sheltered bays and salty marshes of the Dingle Peninsula that make this coastal wilderness perfect for novices.

If you're a complete beginner, the quiet Smerwick Harbour, hemmed in by the bare rocky cliffs of Cloonduane, offers calmer waters perfect for jumping on a board for the first time. The same can be said for the harbor in the town of Dingle—although the waft of fish and chips from the restaurants lining the waterfront may tempt you out of the water sooner than you'd planned. Horseshoe-shaped Brandon Bay, meanwhile, is a good place to hone your skills. Here, you can learn the basics in flat water, and then—once you feel comfortable—test yourself on the gentle waves that roll into the bay. This spot is thought to be one of the best places in the world to windsurf—and riding high on the swell, with the sunlight glittering on the ocean and the green knife-edge of Mount Brandon in the distance, it's easy to see why.

Windsurfer riding the swell just off the coast of the Dingle Peninsula

Hiking

Opportunities for hiking in Europe are endless. That's not hyperbole: 12 long-distance E-paths alone span more than 43,500 miles (70,000 km), from Arctic Norway to southern Cyprus. And that's not to mention the thousands of other trails lacing mountains, tracing coastlines, and linking towns and villages. However far you go, you'll need some stamina—with steep inclines and tricky terrain, these hikes are as challenging to tackle as they are satisfying to complete.

▷ AIGÜESTORTES I ESTANY DE SANT MAURICI NATIONAL PARK, SPAIN

Get off the grid in the Pyrenees by hiking from lush forests to high-mountain plateaus.

Catalonia's only national park feels like a sanctuary: off-limits to private vehicles, its flourishing forests and glacier-carved valleys are the exclusive domain of hikers and cyclists. Crowned by Mulhacen and Veleta, two of Spain's highest mountains, the park is made verdant by the crystalline streams that crisscross its terrain. Embarking along one of the 27 hiking trails here, you'll follow these waterways as they thread into pine forests and between boulder-dotted plains. One of the most gratifying routes is the trail to Sant Maurici Lake. After tramping through meadows and secluded glades, you can revel in sublime mountain views as you cool your weary feet in the water.

Looking out over Sant Maurici Lake in Aigüestortes i Estany de Sant Maurici National Park

△ SAMARIÁ GORGE, CRETE

Descend through "Europe's Grand Canyon"—the most dramatic cleft in Crete's White Mountains.

Bigger isn't always better—but the 10-mile (16 km) long Samariá Gorge, Europe's longest canyon, has beauty as well as brawn. Carved by the river gushing from the Omalós plain down to the Libyan Sea on Crete's southwestern shore, this hefty rift is awe-inspiring indeed—its sheer walls rise some 1,640 ft (500 m) in places, narrowing to just a few yards wide at the bottleneck dubbed Sidherespórtes (Iron Gates). It's not just a rock show, though; you might be lucky enough to spy rare kri-kri—wild Cretan goats with immense curved horns—and in spring, you'll hike among the blooms of iris and white peony. Guaranteed at the end, regardless, are the inviting turquoise waters of the Mediterranean at Agía Rouméli—perfect for a reviving dip.

Hiking alongside a stream through Samariá Gorge, on the Greek island of Crete

Insider Tip

Samariá Gorge is open early May to October, depending on weather (wildflowers are most profuse in the first few weeks of the season). The majority of hikers start soon after dawn to dodge midday heat; consider setting out mid-morning to miss the crowds, overnighting in Agía Rouméli.

The lush green landscape of Glen Coe, one of many famous Scottish sights that can be viewed from the West Highland Way

▽ PUY DE DÔME, FRANCE

Trek the ash-streaked slopes of Puy de Dôme to survey a land forged by ancient volcanoes.

France's Auvergne region is ridged with a chain of slumbering volcanoes, stretching 28 miles (45 km) from north to south. The highest of these is the 4,806 ft (1,465 m) Puy de Dôme, from whose summit you can enjoy the most spectacular views. Some visitors catch a cog railroad there, but hiking the three-hour Chèvres Trail lets you experience the geological drama up close.

Hints of the peak's explosive past lie all around, from the ashy black soil beneath your walking boots to the craggy boulders that stud the blustery plateaus. The trail itself winds through glades of silver birch and muddy meadows, before leading you on a final, muscle-stiffening climb to the top. Your reward for conquering Puy de Dôme? A panorama of cinder cones and velvety green farmland. And remember: there's always the cog railroad, if your legs are too wobbly for the descent.

◁ WEST HIGHLAND WAY, SCOTLAND

Take the high road through the heart of Scotland via lochs, glens, bens, and distilleries.

In simple highlights-per-mile terms, Scotland's oldest and most popular long-distance trail is nigh unbeatable. The sights rack up incrementally over the varied 96-mile (154 km) route, winding north across the Highlands from Glasgow's outskirts to Fort William. There are the shores of Loch Lomond, home to the cave hideout of 18th-century outlaw hero Rob Roy McGregor. There's the bleakly beautiful vastness of Rannoch Moor, and the haunting (and reputedly haunted) vale of Glen Coe, where red deer roam and golden eagles soar. And then there's the bulk of Ben Nevis, Britain's roof, which you'll hike beneath. The path is bookended by two venerable whiskey distilleries—Glengoyne, near the start, and Ben Nevis in Fort William—so you can toast your journey with a couple of wee drams.

Surveying the volcanic landscape of the Auvergne region from the top of Puy de Dôme

"*In simple highlights-per-mile terms, Scotland's oldest and most popular long-distance trail is unbeatable.*"

▷ ACCURSED MOUNTAINS, ALBANIA

Follow ancient trails among the pale karst peaks of far northern Albania, between remote villages steeped in traditional mountain life.

Variously known as the Dinaric Alps, the Albanian Alps and, in the national language, simply Malësia (Highlands), this dramatic limestone massif is most commonly called Bjeshkët e Namuna: "The Accursed Mountains." In summer, when butterflies festoon wildflower meadows like confetti and birds throng the forests, cliffs, and valleys, that moniker seems ill-fitting indeed. But visit high-level settlements still without electricity and cell phone reception, many of them cut off by snow for months each winter, and you'll begin to understand how tough life has always been in these remote reaches.

And visit you should, because the long-isolated valleys of Thethi and Valbona (each at the heart of an eponymous national park) offer sensational trekking, scintillating wildlife, and fascinating cultural insights. The traditions of the Gheg people of this remote region, hidden among forbidding peaks, survived essentially untouched by the waves of invaders and political upheavals that transformed the rest of Albania. Largely self-sufficient lifestyles survive today, much as they have for millennia, based around sheep-herding and growing crops such as corn and plums, the latter used for making *raki* firewater.

Still, the modern world is arriving in the Accursed Mountains, in the form of improved roads (some still 4WD only), simple guesthouses, and, helpfully, increasing numbers of waymarked paths enabling hikers to explore ever farther and higher. The main village in each valley provides a handy base for roaming the trails. Thethi is more traditional, with its wood-shingled church and centuries-old *kulla* (lock-in tower), a legacy of the blood feuds that often flared between clans. Valbona, to the east, is more recently developed but provides equally varied hiking

opportunities. Linking the two is a nameless track over the Valbona pass—just one of many superb trails leading through the peaks here, which are dominated by the 8,839 ft (2,694 m) Mount Jezerca. A host of smaller settlements also offer homestays and camping spots, expanding your walking range further still.

Whether you aim high among the summits, roam through shepherd pastures, or trace streams to tempting swimming holes (such as the spectacular Blue Eye spring), you'll discover a marvelous array of wildlife. You might delve into beech woods prowled by wild boar, bears, and wolves, encounter yellow-blotched black fire salamanders near caves and rivers after rain, or spy chamois and soaring golden eagles among the loftiest crags. And by hiking through these long-isolated uplands, you'll gain a deep appreciation for how people have adapted to live among such raw, untrammeled nature.

∧

Insider Tip

The most thrilling way to approach the Valbona Valley involves a two- to three-hour ferry from Koman to Fierza along Lake Komani. This narrow, twisting, sheer-sided waterway was created by a 1970s hydroelectric project and is now rich in birdlife. A minibus via Bajram Curri can take you the rest of the way.

Above The *kulla*, or lock-in tower, at Thethi
Right Hiking along a narrow path in the Accursed Mountains

Spotter's Guide

Golden Eagle

This raptor, with a wingspan up to 7 ft (2.2 m), can be seen soaring on thermals, awaiting opportunities to snatch young goats or chamois.

Black Woodpecker

The largest woodpecker found in the area, growing over 20 in (50 cm) long, this forest-dweller has striking black plumage offset by its vivid red cap.

Nose-Horned Viper

This beautifully patterned snake, with its dark zigzag back markings, sports a distinctive "horn" at the tip of its nose. Spot it in bushes or on rocky slopes.

Dipper

This plump little bird with white breast and chin can be spotted plunging into streams to forage for invertebrate prey or bobbing up and down on a nearby rock.

HIKING **235**

Dropping into the icy depths with just a swimsuit and hat to stave off the chill is a daunting prospect. But such is the addictive power of the cold that, for many, ice swimming is a way of life. You'll need a good guide if it's your first time, plus plenty of gumption, but the exhilaration afterward will make it all worthwhile.

▷ REYKJAVÍK, ICELAND

Take a freezing dip at Nauthólsvík Geothermal Beach. With handy hot tubs for warming up afterward, it's the perfect place for ice-swimming novices.

Iceland has plenty of hidden swimming holes scattered across its rugged landscape, where hardy locals break the ice and drop into frigid water to get their fix. But you don't necessarily have to venture into the island's remote backcountry to sample ice swimming—instead, head to Nauthólsvík Geothermal Beach. Tucked away on a small inlet, the beach is just a short walk from the center of Reykjavík. The community of welcoming winter swimmers and the excellent waterside facilities—including toasty hot tubs—mean it's a great bet for novice ice swimmers, as well as for those looking for an alternative to Iceland's more tourist-trodden sights. ▶

Diving in to the ice-cold sea at Nauthólsvík Geothermal Beach in Reykjavík

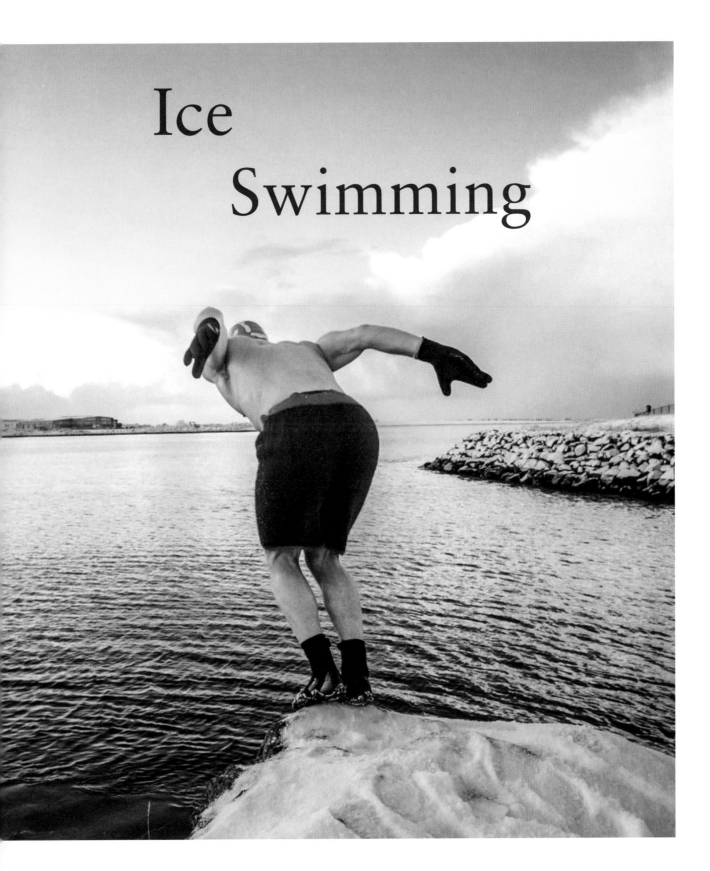

Ice
Swimming

Insider Tip

Keeping the icy wind off your
ears and the water off your
head will make warming up
afterward a lot easier, so invest
in a neoprene hat or pack a
spare woolly hat that you don't
mind getting wet. Neoprene
shoes and gloves will also help
ward off the chill.

As the nights draw in and the temperature plummets, the
sea here drops to as low as 28°F (−2°C), with ice collecting
on its fringes in a frozen sheet. You'll need to pay a small
entrance fee to enter the beach (it's free in summer) before
getting into your swimming attire in the warm changing
area. From there, it's a short, but admittedly chilly, stroll to
the shoreline; if the ice is thick, you may have to wait for the
locals to break it with an ax before you get in. Even if you've
tried ice swimming before, the effect as you enter the water
is still the same—you'll feel a sharp shock all over your body
and won't be able to focus on anything other than your
gasping breath and the hefty punch of the cold as you sink
beneath the lapping waves. Try to slow your breathing down
and focus on taking short breaststrokes.

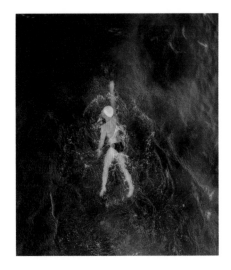

Above Swimming through the icy waters of Nauthólsvík
Right Warming up in one of the cozy hot tubs after a dip
Left Climbing out of the sea at the edge of the beach

Remember: just getting in counts as an achievement, and even the most experienced swimmers can handle only a few minutes before they need to get out. If it's your first time, opt for a quick dunk, listen to local advice, and know your limits—lifeguards are on hand, but staying safe and listening to your body are paramount.

As you emerge back onto the snow-covered beach and head toward the hot tubs, your skin starts to tingle as an endorphin rush takes hold of your body. The larger of the two baths, which are naturally heated using geothermal water, is kept at a delicious 101°F (38.5°C). Sliding in here after a few minutes in freezing water is nothing short of heaven. You might even love it so much that you'll want to repeat the whole process over again.

A Sustainable Development

The sustainable geothermal water that warms the lagoon and hot tubs is pumped from Perlan, the eye-catching water tanks that stand at the top of nearby Oskjuhlid Hill. There are six tanks, each carrying 879,877 gallons (4 million liters) of natural hot water pumped from the Reykir geothermal area. Some of this hot water is also pumped from Perlan into homes across Reykjavík.

▽ MURMANSK, RUSSIA

Follow in the breaststrokes of Russia's toughest
ice swimmers.

Set in a remote corner of northwestern Russia, Murmansk
has a rich ice-swimming history. Its "Walrus Club," now
numbering more than 500 hardy souls, was formed in
1965 by locals eager to expound the benefits of a freezing
dip in Lake Semyonovskoye. The lake's reputation is now
so well established that in 2019 it played host to the
world ice-swimming championships.

You, too, can immerse yourself in this rich tradition
by visiting the small ice pool used by the Walrus Club
members. Steps drop 20 in (50 cm) through the ice and
into the deep, so getting in and out is easy—or at least as
straightforward as it can be when the water temperature
is around 32°F (0°C) and the air temperature even lower.

▷ ROVANIEMI, FINLAND

Plunge into a freezing Finnish lake then take
off the chill in a sauna.

For Finns, ice swimming is part of a wider well-being
ritual that includes warming up in a post-dip sauna. The
extremes of cold and hot have been scientifically shown
to improve the immune system and also leave you with
glowing skin for hours afterward.

In keeping with Finnish tradition, every winter the lakes
near Rovaniemi become hot spots for ice swimming, with
plunge pools carved out of the ice next to permanent
wooden saunas. The walk between the two is usually nice
and short, so there's little time to lose your nerve. Even
better, once you've finished your swim, the heat of the fire
will get you warm within minutes, so you'll be all set for a
second or third dip before getting back into your clothes.

An ice-swimming competition at Lake
Semyonovskoye in Murmansk

"For Finns, ice swimming is part of a wider well-being ritual that includes warming up in a post-dip sauna."

Snorkeling

Few activities transport you so quickly into another world as snorkeling. As you glide above an underwater landscape filled with otherworldly flora and fauna, time slows down and the concerns of the outside world drift away. It is also generally inexpensive and accessible; you don't need to buy fancy equipment, have done training courses, or be super fit. An ability to swim, a mask and snorkel, and a sense of adventure are easily enough to get started.

▷ MAKARSKA RIVIERA, CROATIA

This rugged slice of the Dalmatian Coast offers quality snorkeling straight from the beach.

Backed by the Biokovo mountain range, the 37-mile (60 km) Makarska Riviera is dotted with over a thousand beaches—most of them pebbly—that shelve gently into the Adriatic Sea. In these turquoise waters, you'll find an abundance of coastal marine life, thanks to high environmental standards and an array of underground springs that keep the water clean and biodiverse. Add to this excellent water clarity (due to a lack of sand and sediment) and you have some of Europe's best snorkeling conditions.

From the town of Makarska, head along the coast in either direction and you will come across hundreds of beaches, some blanketing expansive bays, others nestled in tiny coves or edging sweeping headlands. The most popular beaches have facilities such as lifeguards, sun loungers, umbrellas, and toilets, but many others remain in their natural state—the latter are generally the best for snorkeling. Most are sheltered, and there are few strong currents, so the sea is calm—ideal for novice snorkelers and families. Close to the shore, constellations of starfish are scattered across the seabed, solitary octopuses and crabs dart in and out of view, and shoals of tiny multicolor fish move gracefully in unison. Further out, conger eels, groupers, sea cucumbers, and golden sponges can be spotted in the still-clear waters.

One of the standout beaches is Garma Bay, which has a pair of offshore reefs teeming with marine life. Another popular spot is Nugal—flanked by towering cliffs and fragrant pine forests, its rocky shoreline provides a habitat for a host of fish, shellfish, and crustaceans, including herds of delicate seahorses.

Right Exploring the Makarska Riviera
Far right Shoal of brightly colored fish
Below Snorkeling off the Dalmatian Coast

Far left Swimming over the seabed past a shoal of fish
Left One of the shipwrecks found in the Marine Protected Area of Tavolara
Below A family snorkeling in turquoise seas

Insider Tip

The best time to go snorkeling in the Marine Protected Area of Tavolara is between May and October, when the average water temperature is 64–75°F (18–24°C) and water visibility is between 49 ft and 131 ft (15 m and 40 m).

◁ MARINE PROTECTED AREA OF TAVOLARA, SARDINIA, ITALY

Discover an array of sea life and shipwrecks in the limpid waters off northeast Sardinia.

Spread across 58 sq miles (150 sq km) of the crystalline Tyrrhenian Sea, Italy's second largest marine reserve is a haven for snorkelers. Created in 1997, Tavolara is dotted with craggy islands populated by myriad bird species; picture-postcard beaches; and long, rugged peninsulas. Excellent water visibility here—thanks largely to the area's protected status—makes it easy to spot eels slipping out of gloomy crevices, predatory barracudas prowling through fields of seagrass, and graceful loggerhead turtles drifting over the sandy seabed. Meanwhile, the rocky shorelines are home to colonies of shags, sleek, cormorant-like birds who dive below the surface in search of small fish, providing a memorable sight for any snorkelers in the vicinity. There are also several eerie shipwrecks, notably the *Chrisso*, which ran aground on a stormy night in 1974 and now lies broken and semi-submerged in the shallows. Swim over its rusted skeleton, and you'll find a thriving ecosystem of mollusks, crustaceans, and shoals of colorful fish.

Exploring the underwater
landscape off the coast of
the island of Harris

Swimming around
one of the coral reefs
near the Medes Islands

▷ MEDES ISLANDS, SPAIN

Immerse yourself in a thriving marine reserve
just off the sunny Costa Brava.

Once patrolled by pirates and corsairs, the pristine
waters around the Medes Islands now attract snorkelers
eager to explore a conservation area home to more than
600 species. The ecological value of the archipelago,
which lies barely a 1.6 km (mile) off the coast of the town
of L'Estartit, has long been recognized. In 1983, fishing
was restricted here to preserve the diverse flora and
fauna, and seven years later, a more comprehensive
marine reserve was created. The reserve was expanded
in 2010 and now spans more than 2 sq miles (5 sq km) of
the Mediterranean, as well as the islands themselves—no
one is allowed to set foot on them to ensure the nesting
birds that live here are protected.

The impact of these conservation efforts quickly
becomes apparent when you strap on a mask and snorkel,
and start to explore. You'll soon find multicolored coral
reefs sporting elegant fans, bulbous growths, and tubular
protrusions, as well as meadows of seagrass swaying
gently in the currents. These underwater landscapes are
home to sinuous eels, cleverly camouflaged octopuses,
and multitudes of minute fish.

As you move out into deeper waters, keep your eyes
peeled for sleek, menacing barracudas, shoals of black-
and-white-striped sea bream, and dusky groupers—these
slow-moving, wide-mouthed and inquisitive creatures
will sometimes approach snorkelers for a closer look. If
you study the seabed, you might even see a common
stingray gliding gracefully by or—closer to the surface
and with a hefty slice of luck—possibly a pod of playful
bottlenose dolphins.

△ NORTH HARRIS, SCOTLAND

Follow a specially designed snorkeling trail through
the fertile waters of the Outer Hebrides.

The Outer Hebrides may not be the most obvious spot for
snorkeling, but this far-flung archipelago is blessed with
remarkably varied underwater landscapes—which you
can explore on the North Harris Snorkel Trail. Created by
the Scottish Wildlife Trust in 2017, this self-guided route
covers six beaches and bays, with options for both beginners and experienced snorkelers. Marker posts guide you
over sandy seabeds sprinkled with starfish, reefs filled
with slithering sand eels, and forests of kelp patrolled by
silver-streaked pollack. The area is also rich in jellyfish—
although beautiful, some can give painful stings, so keep
your distance. Keep your eye out for species such as the
bell-shaped, eight-armed stalked jellyfish, and the giant
lion's mane, with its shaggy mass of long tentacles.

> **"** *This far-flung archipelago is
> blessed with remarkably varied
> underwater landscapes.* **"**

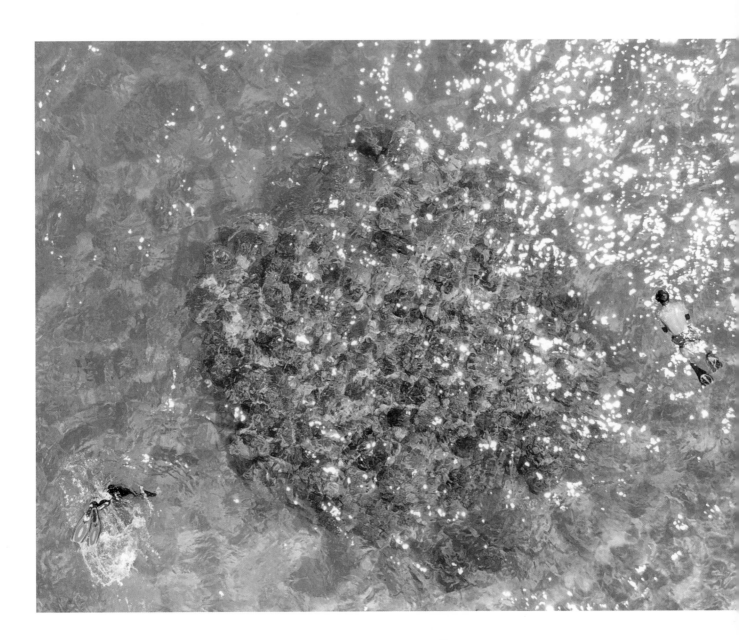

Bottlenose Dolphin

Growing up to 13 ft (4 m) in length and living for 60 years or more, this species is one of the most intelligent animals on the planet.

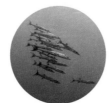

Barracuda

A fearsome predator armed with fanglike teeth, barracudas are long, sleek, silvery-gray and capable of speeds of more than 25 mph (40 km/h).

Dusky Grouper

A large, barrel-shaped fish that can weigh up to 110 lb (50 kg) and measure up to 5 ft (1.5 m). It uses its huge mouth to swallow its prey whole.

Common Stingray

Dark-brown to jet-black in color, common stingrays are found on the seabed, where they often bury themselves in sediment as a disguise while they hunt.

Index

Acknowledgments

Dorling Kindersley would like to thank the following authors for their words:

Soraya Abdel-Hadi is an award-winning writer and artist, focused on sustainability, nature, and adventure travel. When she isn't horse riding, hiking, or biking, she is a climbing instructor and organizes sailing voyages all over the world.

Helen Abramson, ex-Rough Guides editor and travel writer, is a self-proclaimed adrenaline junkie. Five years ago, she fell hook, line, and sinker for kitesurfing. Now a Creative Manager at UNICEF UK, Helen spends her vacations searching for kiting spots without the crowds and seeking out the nearest thrill-seeking activities.

Ruth Allen is an author and ecopsychotherapist based in the Peak District, UK. She specializes in nature-based therapy, nature connection, and working with body and movement. In her spare time, she likes to adventure on foot and by bike and has a fondness for the cold north and islands of the Atlantic. In 2018, she made the assumed first solo and unsupported run across the Bosnian Mountains.

Julianna Barnaby is a London-based travel writer and founder of the award-winning sites The Discoveries Of and London x London. When she's not searching out London's most unusual spots, she can often be found road tripping around remote locations in search of outdoor adventures—recent favorites include the Lofoten Islands in Norway and the Atacama Desert in Chile.

Sophie Blackman graduated with a degree in English Literature before becoming a nonfiction editor in London, where she creates books for both children and adults. She is a keen traveler, walker, and mushroom forager and has previously contributed to the DK Eyewitness guides on San Francisco and the Dordogne.

Paul Bloomfield is a writer and photographer specializing in active adventures, wildlife, and history. He's cycled, hiked, kayaked, rafted, and run thousands of miles across six continents, writing travel features for newspapers, magazines, websites, and books, including *The Telegraph*, *The Times*, *Wanderlust*, *National Geographic Traveller*, and *BBC Wildlife*.

Keith Drew, a former Managing Editor at Rough Guides, writes about the wilder regions of Europe for *The Telegraph* and *BRITAIN Magazine* among various others publications. He is the cofounder of family-travel website Lijoma. com, a curated selection of inspirational itineraries that includes exciting destinations like Iceland, Croatia, the Scottish Highlands, and Snowdonia.

Sam Haddad lives in Brighton, UK, with her family. She is an award-winning writer and experienced editor specializing in adventure, travel, and action sports, and her work has appeared in *The Guardian*, *The Times*, and *1843 Magazine*, among others. You can keep up with her on Twitter: @shhhaddad.

Anita Isalska is a British writer and editor based in California. Anita writes about outdoor travel, European history, and offbeat adventures, focusing on France and Central Europe. When she isn't researching stories, Anita splits her time between skiing, cycling, and mountain hikes. Read her stuff on www.anitaisalska.com.

Joshua Kian is a writer and outdoor enthusiast who finds inspiration in nature. From climbing and hiking to wild camping and bike touring, he is passionate about promoting a sustainable future through emission-free outdoor pursuits, including his current England-to-India bike tour.

Seth McBride is an editor and writer for *New Mobility*, a magazine for active wheelchair users, and a lifelong lover of outdoor adventure. Whether it's long handcycle tours abroad or weekend mountain biking or hiking excursions, he's a firm believer that the world is best explored under your own power.

Shafik Meghji is an award-winning travel writer, journalist, and coauthor of more than 40 guidebooks for Rough Guides and DK Eyewitness. He writes for *BBC Travel*, *Wanderlust*, and Adventure.com, among others, and talks about travel on TV, radio, and podcasts. He can be found on Twitter and Instagram: @ShafikMeghji.

Richard Mellor started out providing PR for vacation firms but soon realized that he preferred writing about exotic places than showing them to journalists, and swapped sides. Now a London-based travel writer, his favorite adventures involve seclusion, slow-paced outdoor pursuits, some wildlife watching, and a dose of wellness.

Rachel Mills is a freelance writer and editor based by the sea in Kent. She is a regular contributor to DK Eyewitness, Rough Guides, *The Telegraph*, and loveEXPLORING.com and is also an expert in sustainable, responsible tourism. Follow her: @rachmillstravel.

Joe Minihane is an author and travel journalist based in Brighton, UK. His book, *Floating: A Life Regained*, charts a journey swimming around the UK in a bid to deal with anxiety. His travel writing has appeared in *The Guardian*, *The Sunday Times*, and CNN Travel.

Lizzie Pook is an award-winning journalist specializing in adventure and wildlife travel. She has ventured to some of the furthest reaches of the planet, from the trans-Himalayas – in search of snow leopards—to the vast, uninhabited east coast of Greenland. She writes for *The Guardian*, *The Telegraph*, and *The Times*, among others.

Daniel Stables is a travel writer based in the UK. He has written or contributed to more than 30 travel books, on destinations ranging from North America to Southeast Asia, and is a regular contributor to leading travel magazines. You can find more of his work at danielstables.co.uk or on Twitter: @DanStables.

Sarah Stirling is a British adventure writer, currently living off-grid in a house-bus. Her solar-powered words appear in a range of publications, from broadsheets to travel books. Her first book, *Rewild Your Life*, is out now. You can find out more about Sarah on her website sarahstirling.com and on Instagram: @sarah_stirling.

Peter Watson is a photographer, writer, and founder of outdoor travel blog Atlas & Boots. A keen trekker and climber, he can usually be found on the trails of the Greater Ranges. He's visited over 80 countries and is currently focused on climbing the seven summits—the highest mountain on every continent.

The publisher would like to thank the following for their kind permission to reproduce their data:

190 Auttila, Miina & Niemi, Marja & Skrzypczak, Teresa & Viljanen, Markku & Kunnasranta, Mervi. (2014). Estimating and Mitigating Perinatal Mortality in the Endangered Saimaa Ringed Seal (Phoca hispida saimensis) in a Changing Climate. Annales Zoologici Fennici. 51. 526-534. 10.5735/086.051.0601.

The publisher would like to thank Nanna Dís for supplying images of Iceland for the Ice Swimming section, plus the following for their kind permission to reproduce their photographs:

Key: a-above; b-below/bottom; c-centre; f-far; l-left; r-right; t-top

4Corners: Pete Goding 199bl; Michael Howard 159tr; Ben Pipe 235tl; Maurizio Rellini 130-31; Luigi Vaccarella 5t.

Alamy Stock Photo: AGAMI Photo Agency / Daniele Occhiato 155cb; agefotostock / Hoffmann Photography 73crb, / Jörgen Larsson 81cra, / Xavier Subias 114clb; Agencja Fotograficzna Caro / Teich 144br; Montserrat Alejandre 143ca; John Angerson 118tl; Arctic Images / Ragnar Th Sigurdsson 239tl; Art World 154clb; Arterra Picture Library / Arndt Sven-Erik 177crb, / De Meester Johan 31tr; Ivan Batinic 240cra; Craige Bevil 230br; Biosphoto / Frederic Desmette 208tc, / Gerard Soury 247crb; Blickwinkel / F. Hecker 40crb; Blue Planet Archive WPO 62-63c; Sergi Boixader 186tl; Petr Bonek 217tc; Buiten-Beeld / Jelger Herder 14cb (lizard); Benoit Cappronnier 155cb (Boar); Cavan Images 106-07c, / Patrick Kunkel 183tc; Peter Cavanagh 73cb (Dursey); Cristian Cestaro 142crb; Joanna Clegg 171clb; Chris Cole 204-05; Christopher Cook 170cb (Chough); Matjaz Corel 114-15; CTK / Vaclav Pancer 20bl; Cultura Creative Ltd / George Karbus Photography 170crb; Mark Delete 132; Goncalo Diniz 203bc; Reinhard Dirscherl 247cb; Dave Donaldson 94t; Cody Duncan 45tr; Peter Eastland 207br; Alex Ekins 128-29c; Alex Fieldhouse 235crb; Tony French 109tr; Bob Gibbons 206-07c; Tim Graham 51tl; HelloWorld Images 80cb; Hemis. fr / Franck Guiziou 36, 233br, / Jacques Sierpinski 149bl, / Jean-Franтois Hagenmuller 177tr, / Patrice Hauser 196bl; Mark Hicken 97tl; Lee Hudson 170clb; Ilkka Uusitalo photos 88-89; Image Professionals GmbH / Klaus Fengler 44clb; Image Source / Marco Simoni 117; imageBROKER / Wolfgang Diederich 160br,/ Guenter Fischer 207cra, / Stefan Huwiler 14clb, / Alexander Schnurer 247clb, / Frank Schneider 58, / Martin Siepmann 219tr, / Siepmann 191tc, / Winfried Wisniewski 133clb; incamerastock / ICP 199t; Brian Jannsen 22; Johner Images 81cla; Frans Lemmens 41br; Andrew Lloyd 216bl; David Lyons 24-25b; markferguson2 72tr; McPhoto / Schaef 235cb; Jerome Murray - CC 122cb (Skuas); Nature Picture Library 9, 61t, / Paul Harcourt Davies 207crb, / Danny Green 30tl, / Wild Wonders of Europe, / Lilja 206crb; Marketa Novakova 103br; Kasia Nowak 73clb; PA Images / Ciaran McCrickard 198clb; Michalis Palis 207tr; Ville Palonen 27b; Anthony Pierce 189clb; Radharc Images / JoeFox Liverpool 200tl; Johannes Rigg 73cb; RJH_IMAGES 21crb; Robertharding / Christian Kober 224bl, / David Pickford 85t, / Laura Grier 52tl, / Peter Barritt 28br; Rowan Romeyn 135b; RooM the Agency / KevinCarr 96clb; Katharine Rose 38t; Pere Sanz 143tc; Malcolm Schuyl 26clb; Scottish.Photography 25tl; Smharperphotography 122crb; Philip Smith 40cb; Stock Italia 91; Stockimo / Kaisa Mikkola 96t, / Ray Wood 113clb; Stocktrek Images, Inc. / Alan Dyer 142cb; Andy Sutton 177tl; The Landscaper 170tl; The Photolibrary Wales 112tc; Tierfotoagentur / D. M. Sheldon 14crb; travellinglight 16br; Unlisted Images, Inc. / Fotosearch 170cb; WaterFrame_dpr 235clb; Robin Weaver 112tc (Arddu); Westend61 GmbH / Alun Richardson 223c; Kevin Wheal 38bl; Fred van Wijk 122clb; Xinhua / Apostolos Domalis 76tl; ZUMA / Andrey Pronin 240bl.

Association Touristique Aigle-Leysin-Col Des Mosses: José Crespo 212-13.

AWL Images: ClickAlps 86.

Andrew Burr: 44-45.

Titi Ceara: "*Shepherd and the Donkey Tekir*" by Titi Ceara, brass sculpture, 2004 119clb.

Depositphotos Inc: 8tik 176tl; happyalex 212clb; pyty 92-93b.

Discover The Nature - Outdoor Events ®: www.discoverthenature.com 172.

Dreamstime.com: Alkan2011 228-29b; Nuno Almeida 156, 158tl; Anyaberkut 227; Fokke Baarssen 84br; Richard Banary 165br; Beriliu 71br; Musat Christian 155clb; Henner Damke 192tr; Deaddogdodge 124tl; Diadis 16bl; Randy Van Domselaar 32clb; Andrei Efimov 220-21; Eric Rebmann Paris Estate Services 177br;

Eudaemon 40t; F8grapher 160bl; Patrik Forsberg 120-21; Sven Hansche 82tl; Tatsiana Hendzel 54; Henrimartin 121cra; Dennis Jacobsen 31crb; Ilyas Kalimullin 60cra; Kaprik 217b; Kloeg008 33tc; Kuba 133cb (warbler); Dejan Kuralt 126-27; Steve Lagreca 152-53b; Lcrms7 231t; Makasanaphoto 165tl; Mariagroth 20tr, 21l; Davide Marzotto 174tl; Michalludwiczak 149tr; Rosen Minchev 12br; Nataliya Nazarova 93tr; Mihai Neacsu 164-65b; Vyacheslav Opalev 133cb; Martin Pelanek 235cb (viper); Björkdahl Per 80cb (Gålö); Peter Kováč 70; Poike2017 83; Scott Prokop 190crb; Pytyczech 93tl; Manuel Ribeiro 203bl; George Robertson 197; Jonas Rönnbro 180tr; Ronstik 6-7; Salajean 110-11; Saletomic 134tl; Yvonne Stewart 61bl; T.w. Van Urk 116br; Voyagerix 98tl; Charlotte Wilkins 193cb (Fin); Wirestock 180crb; Vladislav Zhukov 47.

© Foundation Conservation Carpathia / Georgiana & Mihai Catan: 31tl.

Getty Images: 500px / Andrew Barrett 112tr, / Gerard Autran 177cra, / Inna Hoerfurter 64bl; 500Px Plus / Cristian Moldovan 247cb (Barracuda), / Dmitry Fomin 222tl, / David Sieb 150-51, / Priit Einbaum 73t, / Seppo Ulmanen 191tr,/ Rich Wiltshire 98br, 144tl; AFP / Nikolay Doychinov 119br, / Jonathan Nackstrand 201br, / Miguel Medina 178bl, 179t, / Philippe Lopez 106tl; Aurora Photos / Alexandra Simone 109tc; Cavan Images 97tr, 98bl; Corbis Documentary / Atlantide Phototravel 33tl; Corbis Sport /

Stefan Matzke - sampics 158cla, 158-59c; Cultura / Roberto Peri 244-45b; De Agostini / DEA / ICAS94 164tl; DigitalVision / Chris Hepburn 112tl,/ Alan Novelli 112b, / Andre Schoenherr 42-43; E+ / Flavio Vallenari 140crb; EyeEm / Charlotte Hall 180cb, / Hrvoje Gradecak 243tr, / Artem Khaklin 37cra,/ Fabian Krause 242-43b, / Rovena Kortoçi 56tl,/ Daniela Paragone 27tl, / Rami Salle 27tc; Christopher Furlong 113bl; Gamma-Rapho / Michael Serraillier 92tl; Johner Images 79, 80-81t, 81tl, 180cb (Bilberry), 181tr, 224tr; Erik Leonsson 180clb; Lumi Images / P. J. Robertson 5bl,/ Romulic-Stojcic 243tc; Moment / Chase Dekker Wild-Life Images 28-29, / Andrea Comi 16tl, 100, / © Santiago Urquijo 57r, / Elva Etienne 182-83b, 183tr, / Enrique Mesa Photography 141, / Ernesto r. Ageitos 38br, / Francesco Riccardo Iacomino 123, / Michael J. Cohen, Photographer 96crb, / K.Muller 142cb (Orion), / Harald Nachtmann 25br, / Jacky Parker Photography 208tl, / Jean-Philippe Tournut 13, / Alexander Spatari 68bl, / Amy Shore 94bl, / Maria Swärd 80clb, / Natapong Supalertsophon 52bl, / Pat Gaines 142clb, / photo by Pam Susemiehl 62clb, / Photograph by Paul Greeves 232, / Richard McManus 96cb (Pine Martens),Tsvetomir Hristov 182clb, / by wildestanimal 135tc, 192, 193crb; Moment Open / by wildestanimal 61br, / Fabrizio Moglia 33b, / John Lawson; Belhaven 40cb (Wrack), / Sandra Standbridge 57tl, / www. deirdregregg.com 200b; NurPhoto / Krystian

Dobuszynski 133crb, / Ascent Xmedia / Milo Zanecchia 223tc, / Graham Lucas Commons 15cla, / Milo Zanecchia / Ascent Xmedia 64t, / Peter Cade 199br; Science Photo Library / Mark Garlick 51crb; Gerard Soury 193cb; Stone / Ascent Xmedia / Milo Zanecchia 222clb, 222-23t, / Mike Hill 48, / Silvia Otte 241, / Tyler Stableford 103tl; The Image Bank / Ben Welsh 160tl, / Nancy Brown 173cra; Universal Images Group / Arterra / Sven-Erik Arndt 67tr, / REDA&CO 148tl, / Massimo Piacentino 123tl, / Mauro Spanu 228tr; Westend61 2-3, 14-15t, 16tr, 64br.

iStockphoto.com: AvGusT174 146; cesa53rone 190-91; Richard Constantinoff 124tr; E+ / Freder 193cr, / golfer2015 125br, / lechatnoir 66-67c, / Mediterranean 108-09b. / Sjo 135tr, / Stefonlinton 96cb, / wingmar 229br; FilippoBacci 144tr; master2 34-35; Kseniya_Milner 187; samael334 69; Schroptschop 142-43t; Travel Wild 244tc; TZU-HAN-YU 50.

Sheila Ivison: 188.

Kiur Kaasik: 184-85.

Titouan Le Roux: 154-55t.

Viktor Lyagushkin / phototeam.pro: 194-95.

David Morse: 104.

Nevidio Canyoning (www. nevidio-canyoning.com): 76-77c.

ÖTZTAL TOURISMUS (www. oetztal.com): © Area 47 / Rudi Wyhlidal 74.

Outdoor Recreation Northern Ireland: MountainBikeNI.com 11cla, 214-15.

Picfair.com: Sergey Grachev 10; Steve Milne 52tr.

Reykjavík Grapevine / Nanna Dís: 236-37, 238, 239tr.

Robert Harding Picture Library: Marcos Ferro 162-63; Christian Kober 52br; Michel Rauch 155crb.

Scottish Wildlife Trust: Chris Jones 246tl.

Shutterstock.com: Jonas Abdo 129tr; Ilmi Aulia 247tl; Bildagentur Zoonar GmbH 31cr; Costin Boerescu 118-19t; Richard Cavalleri 18t, 18br; Ecuadorpostales 224br; Stefano Garau 244tl; Gorodisskij 102-03c; hybridimages 5br; Kletr 217tr; kovop58 71tl; Panagiotis Mavrakis 63br; Mikadun 166-67; moreimages 45cra; Nenad Basic 107br; novak.elcic 77crb; Jens Ottoson 153tr; Jarmo Piironen 98tr; PJWphoto 94br; Prometheus72 224tl; pulsatilla 144bl; goran_safarek 14cb; Janis Smits 160tr; Calin Stan 124b; Try_my_best 239crb; Tsuguliev 180tl; Ondra Vacek 46tl; VLADIMIR_5 209tl.

SuperStock: Hemis / Berthier Emmanuel 51tr; imageBROKER / Christian Vorhofer 174-75, Look-foto 69tr; Minden Pictures / BIA / Richard Steel 122cb, / Hans Overduin 193clb, Pantheon / Bob GibbonsPanth 40clb; Pixtal 80crb; Robertharding / Jordan Banks 15tl; Westend61 / Egmont Strigl 235tr.

Surf in Comporta: 202-03t.

T.Loubere: 211.

tyf: Mother Goose Films Ltd / (https: / / www. mothergoosefilms.co.uk /) 168-69, 170cla, 170-71t.

Unsplash: CHUTTERSNAP 178br.

VisitOSLO / Didrick Stenersen: 210bl.

Woodland Trust: 208b.

You & Yours: 218.

Zip World: 138-39t.

Zipline Croatia: 136.

Zipline Stoderzinken (www. zipline.at): Christoph Huber 138bl.

Cover images:

Front and Spine: **Daniel Weissenhorn:** Instagram: @daniel_weissenhorn.

Back: **Dreamstime.com:** Sven Hansche bc; **Getty Images:** DigitalVision / Andre Schoenherr bl; Moment / Francesco Riccardo Iacomino cr; Photodisc / Peter Cade tl; **Shutterstock. com:** Gorodisskij c; kovop58 cl; Tsuguliev br; **SuperStock:** imageBROKER / Christian Vorhofer tr; Robertharding / Jordan Banks tc.

For further information see: www.dkimages.com

Project Editor Elspeth Beidas
Editor Rachel Laidler
US Editor Jennette ElNaggar
Senior Designers Laura O'Brien, Ben Hinks
Proofreader Kathryn Glendenning
Indexer Hilary Bird
Picture Researchers Harriet Whitaker, Sumita Khatwani, Vagisha Pushp
Senior Production Editor Jason Little
DTP Designer Tanveer Zaidi
Technical Prepress Manager Tom Morse
Production Controller Rebecca Parton
Production Manager Pankaj Sharma
Managing Editor Hollie Teague
Managing Art Editor Bess Daly
Art Director Maxine Pedliham
Publishing Director Georgina Dee

First American Edition, 2021
Published in the United States by DK Publishing
1450 Broadway, Suite 801, New York, NY 10018

Copyright © 2021 Dorling Kindersley Limited
DK, a Division of Penguin Random House LLC
21 22 23 24 25 10 9 8 7 6 5 4 3 2 1
001-325112-Sep/2021

A catalog record for this book
is available from the Library of Congress.
ISBN 978-0-7440-4225-2

DK books are available at special discounts when purchased in
bulk for sales promotions, premiums, fund-raising, or educational
use. For details, contact: DK Publishing Special Markets,
1450 Broadway, Suite 801, New York, NY 10018
SpecialSales@dk.com

Printed and bound in China

For the curious
www.dk.com

This book was made with Forest Stewardship Council ™ certified
paper—one small step in DK's commitment to a sustainable future.
For more information go to www.dk.com/our-green-pledge

The rapid rate at which the world is changing is constantly
keeping the DK Eyewitness team on our toes. While we've
worked hard to ensure that this edition of *Outdoor Europe* is
accurate and up-to-date, we know that trails are altered,
routes can become impassable, places close and new ones
pop up in their stead. So, if you notice we've got something
wrong or left something out, we want to hear about it. Please
get in touch at travelguides@dk.co.uk